Jesus, Prophecy, and the Middle East

Jesus, Prophecy, and the Middle East

Dr. Anis A. Shorrosh

THOMAS NELSON PUBLISHERS
Nashville • Camden • New York

Second printing, 1982

Unless otherwise noted, all Scripture quotations are from the New American Standard Bible, © The Lockman Foundation 1960, 1962, 1963, 1968, 1971, 1972, 1973, 1975, and are used by permission.

Scripture quotations marked TLB are from *The Living Bible* (Wheaton, Ill.: Tyndale House Publishers, 1971) and are used by permission.

Scripture quotations marked NKJB-NT are from The New King James Bible-New Testament. Copyright © 1979, Thomas Nelson, Inc., Publishers.

Scripture quotations marked KJV are from the King James Version of the Bible.

Published in Nashville, Tennessee, by Thomas Nelson, Inc., Publishers and distributed in Canada by Lawson Falle, Ltd., Cambridge, Ontario.

Printed in the United States of America.

Library of Congress Cataloging in Publication Data

Shorrosh, Anis.
  Jesus, prophecy, and the Middle East.

  Bibliography: p. 143
  1. Bible—Prophecies.   I. Title.
BS647.2.S53   220.1'5   81–923
ISBN 0–8407–5764–6   AACR2

To my dearest friend, wise counselor,
capable colleague, my faithful wife,
Nell;

and to my wonderful children,
Salam, Paul, Steve, and Victoria;

whose abiding love, real understanding, and consistent praying
continues to sustain me as we serve Jesus at home and away
from home; and to the members of our association whose
faithful and prayerful support enables our ministry to reach the
entire world with the gospel.

Contents

Introduction

Ever since it was my privilege to preach for the first time in chapel at the New Orleans Baptist Theological Seminary on December 16, 1966, God has nurtured my dream of writing this book on prophecy. Now that it is done I offer praise to God and acknowledge my debt to those without whose help this work would have been impossible.

No author, great or small, can bring out a significant book without consulting numerous other authors and their works. While I have made a sincere effort to credit my sources in the bibliographic notes at the close of this book, I know that the notes are not complete in every respect. I am indebted to others for their valuable insights.

Because my travels took me across the nation and around the world while writing this book, no one typist could prepare the manuscript in its entirety. Several church secretaries assisted in typing the chapters in their original form. To them, whose names God knows and whose efforts He will reward, I say "Thanks."

A very special word of appreciation goes to Elaine Hedgepath, a God-sent personal secretary. Her sincere love for Jesus, her knowledge of God's Word, and her extraordinary typing talent made my dream of this book a reality.

Finally, I am grateful to God for bringing me to the home of Dr. Hal D. Bennett in Graceville, Florida in February 1979. In the providence of God, Dr. Bennett served in the vital function of editor for the first edition of this book. My grateful appreciation goes also to Wm. Carey Moore for his assistance in updating this present edition.

I have diligently sought to bring this work to the public because of my deep interest in my native land of Palestine and the tremendous worldwide concern with current happenings in the Middle East. I offer it with the special prayer that the Lord will use what I have written to illuminate the issues and inspire the reader to seek the Lord Jesus whose coming again will bring order out of chaos and clarity out of confusion.

Maranatha!

Anis A. Shorrosh, D. Min.
Daphne, Alabama

Jesus,
Prophecy,
and the
Middle East

1

Prophecy Fever

The Lord is not slow about His promise, as some count slowness, but is patient toward you, not wishing for any to perish but for all to come to repentance. But the day of the Lord will come like a thief, in which the heavens will pass away with a roar and the elements will be destroyed with intense heat, and the earth and its works will be burned up. Since all these things are to be destroyed in this way, what sort of people ought you to be in holy conduct and godliness, looking for and hastening the coming of the day of God, on account of which the heavens will be destroyed by burning, and the elements will melt with intense heat! But according to His promise we are looking for new heavens and a new earth, in which righteousness dwells.

(2 Pet. 3:9-13)

An aged Christian man sought me out while I was in India in the late 1970s. This native of Poona thought that since I was from Nazareth and had lived in Jerusalem, I would know the answers to his questions. On the piece of paper he handed me were twenty-one questions—"When will Jesus come?" "Where will He come first?" "Will He be in the clouds?" "Will He land in Jerusalem or in Damascus as the Muslims affirm?"—all concerned with the second coming of Christ. I quickly told him that I appreciated his confidence, yet the Lord had not put me on the time committee—only the preparation committee!

Though this brother's questions took me by surprise, his eager expectation was not out of the ordinary. Everywhere there is a sense of the apocalyptic. To the believer who is walking with his Lord, there is an eager expectation of the blessed return of the Lord Jesus Christ. To the unconverted, the times in which we live bear the scent of doom. As the year A.D. 2000 approaches, the problems of life on this planet are mounting in number and complexity.

Even as society entered the 1980s the signs were ominous. Walter Cronkite, the respected newscaster, expressed a gloomy outlook for the new decade. He identified "four horsemen" of the modern apocalypse: world population, hunger, pollution, and nuclear proliferation. Reporting on Mr. Cronkite's address, *USA Today* headlined the story "Apocalypse Now?"[1] An article in the June 1980 issue of *Futurist* magazine listed four matters of "grave concern" similar to the ones pinpointed by Mr. Cronkite: the arms race, the sticky triangle of population-resources-environment, the fragile economic situation, and quality of life. Its title said it all—"Doomsday Clock: Mankind near Midnight."[2] Weighed down by uncertainties and threats to survival, man cries out for an answer, a deliverer, a supernatural intervention.

True, almost every generation since Christ has considered itself the "end-time generation," but the conditions facing us in the twilight of the twentieth century are unique. While world population climbs toward 4.5 billion, on its way (some say) to 8 billion by A.D. 2015, the earth's resources appear to be running out. But the singular element that injects terror into the future is the awesome power of nuclear arms. Reports like the following, describing an ABC television documentary aired in October 1980, are not uncommon:

A single 20 megaton Soviet bomb dropped on downtown Boston would create heat glares 2,000 times the temperature on the surface of the sun, causing all structures within a mile and a half radius to evaporate, incinerating everyone in downtown Boston and killing almost all within 20 miles from the force of the blast; residents of Martha's Vineyard, 75 miles away, would expire from one wash of radiation.[3]

Taking all of this into consideration, the questions of the man from India do not appear strange or extraordinary at all.

We need to know how to read the signs of the times so that we can do what is needful and expedient. No one, however, has all the answers. While they are to be found in the Word of God, there always has been and is a variance in interpretation of these end-time events. Using the prophetic statements of the Old and New Testaments as sources we will examine these "last days" and the events surrounding the second coming of our Lord. The discussion centers on the Middle East, for there God has acted in history and there He again is to work in fulfillment of prophecy. We will seek to find meaning in the events of the Middle East as they are seen in the light of the prophecies. Only as we understand the Word of God will our response and behavior be according to God's will.

Helping God Fulfill Prophecy

Unfortunately, many of us react to prophetic truth in the wrong way. In 1969 an overzealous Australian decided he would help God fulfill prophecy by setting fire to the revered Al-Aqsa Mosque in Jerusalem. Both the Al-Aqsa Mosque and the more imposing Mosque of Omar, also called the Dome of the Rock, rest on the Temple Mount in Jerusalem. Many believe these structures must be removed to make room for a new Jewish temple on the ancient site of King Solomon's temple.

The only result of the young man's taking these events into his hands was the accusation of the angry Muslims of

Jerusalem that Israel's fire fighters were too slow in extinguish-
ing the fire. After his trial the man was placed in an Israeli
mental hospital and the mosque renovated. For the next three
years no non-Muslims were allowed to enter the mosque, and
when the ban was lifted the temple guards were edgy. A
woman merely opening her purse to get a handkerchief could
cause guards to come running and conduct a search for bombs.

Others have tried to set the date for the return of Christ. In
a little known book, *Forty Future Wonders of Scripture
Prophecy,* the Reverend M. Baxter promised that Christ would
descend on the Mount of Olives on May 2, 1929 or April 9,
1931—at three o'clock! I. R. Dean, in *The Time of the End,*
instructed prophecy buffs to expect the Rapture in 1922. Still
nothing happened. It was the same when William Miller,
known as the founder of the Adventists, misled hundreds of
sincere believers into thinking Christ would come to earth in
"about 1843."

A few years ago a man was handing out stenciled sheets
of paper in Montgomery, Alabama. The announcement said
that he had seen a divine vision concerning the prophecy of
Daniel, declaring that the Dome of the Rock would be destroyed in 1973.

"To be exact," the man said, "it will happen in September and to be more exact, it will be the twenty-third of
September." Then, after elaborate explanations the man added,
"P.S. If these prophecies do not come to pass as I
indicated, you all will know that I misunderstood the
prophecy." At least he was honest. Others have not been so
willing to admit that they could be wrong.

Believing that the Rapture is imminent, the North Hollywood First Assembly of God in California recently drew up a
set of contingency by-laws to become effective immediately
after the Rapture. Normally a person must be a member of the
congregation three years before he is qualified to serve in a
leadership position. But the new rules, which go into effect at

the Rapture, permit members to be elected to leadership posts after six months in the church. Even if you do not agree with this church's interpretation of the Rapture and the last days, you will have to admit that they are serious about putting their beliefs into action.

Books on Prophecy

Perhaps there is no stronger indication of the church's rising preoccupation with future events than the flood of books on the subject now being published. Prophecy titles are snapped up by the thousands—some by the millions. *The Late Great Planet Earth,* written by Hal Lindsey, has now sold nearly twenty million copies and has been made into a successful commercial movie. To a great extent this book started the tremendous prophecy fever of more recent years. I commend it to my readers because it is one of the few books on the subject that God has used to lead people to Jesus Christ as Savior and Lord. Lindsey has also written other books on related themes.

For weeks in 1979 the serious fictional title *The Third World War: August 1985,* by General Sir John Hackett, was on best seller lists in the United States. Thomas Nelson Publishers released four books on prophecy in 1979—*Israel's Final Holocaust* by Jack Van Impe, *Is This the Last Century?* by David Webber and Noah Hutchings, *The Mid-East Peace Puzzle* by Hilton Sutton and Zola Levitt, and *World War III and the Destiny of America* by Charles R. Taylor.

Zola Levitt, a beloved Jewish Christian whom I met a few years ago, has also co-authored with Dr. Thomas McCall the book *Countdown to Rapture*.

David Wilkerson, author of *The Cross and the Switchblade,* wrote *The Vision* a number of years ago, predicting the signs that would come on earth in these days. About that same time, John E. Walvoord wrote *The Blessed Hope and the Tribulation* and Tim LaHaye wrote *The Beginning of the End.*

Salem Kirban, an American whose parents immigrated from Lebanon, has authored numerous books, including *666, I Predict, Guide to Survival,* and *The Day Israel Dies!* More recently Jim McKeever's *Christians Will Go Through the Tribulation* has been followed by his commentary on the book of Revelation. And a non-religious publisher, Macmillan, published *Endtime: The Doomsday Catalogue* in 1980. My own little book, *The Fig Tree,* has been warmly received, making it necessary to issue a second printing.

Films With Prophetic Themes

Simultaneous with what I call a "prophecy fever" in books, there has been a stream of motion pictures that relate to prophetic themes. The film "His Land," produced by the Billy Graham Evangelistic Association, was probably the biggest success of them all. This happy, colorful movie was even adopted by El Al, Israel's airline, for showing on its transoceanic flights. Church people were intrigued with its reporting of fulfilled prophecy in Palestine, the founding of the nation Israel, and the return of millions of Jews to their ancient homeland.

Other evangelical films have received wide circulation, mostly in the churches across America. Their names suggest their prophetic content—"The Return," "The Rapture," "Thief in the Night," "Distant Thunder," "The Temple," "The Road to Armageddon," and "The Vision," a film version of Wilkerson's book.

Of course the television networks and Hollywood have realized the commercial value of films with a prophetic theme. A few years ago two movies about the Antichrist—"Omen" and "Omen II"—were very popular, and more recently "Apocalypse Now" attracted great attention. It actually had little to do with biblical prophecy, but its name suggests a biblical theme. "Apocalypse" is another word for the New Testament's most profound prophetic book, Revelation.

No Place for Sensationalism

I am glad to see the eagerness among God's people for Christian teaching. With the wide usage of cassette recordings, the messages of the prophetic teachers are no longer heard only by their audiences at conferences and banquets. Now most every Christian is within reach of good prophetic teaching, either recorded or live, and this should assist every one of us in contemplating Christ's return with joyful expectation. We can echo, "even so, come, Lord Jesus!"

However, prophecy can tempt people to concentrate on subjects instead of Jesus. While trying to understand the prophetical passages in the Bible, some readers tend to base their faith on an interpretation of the Holy Spirit, of doctrine, or of prophecy. It is of utmost importance that we keep our faith in balance. These are good things in their place, but they are not the essence of Christianity. Are we candid enough to admit that there may be biblical support for views other than our own? Will we be disappointed if our views don't come to pass? And if they do not occur, are we setting ourselves up, needlessly, for embarrassment and disillusionment?

We run the risk, if we do not keep a proper balance, of discrediting the gospel writers and their witness, plus seriously shaking the faith of other Christians, particularly those who are not mature enough to understand these matters. Sensationalism is unnecessary. Judgment is coming, but biblical writers such as the apostle Peter motivate us to repentance and godly living (see 1 Pet. 4:7,8). We should not be overly excited like the people at Thessalonica to whom Paul had to write a second letter in order to calm them down (see 2 Thess. 2).

I have found that in the church there are those who have

their favorite prophetic teachers, and thus they uncritically accept whatever their teacher has to say. Many prophecy students accept Hal Lindsey's book as the ultimate in understanding prophecy. Actually my friend Hal may not be right. He expects the coming of the Lord in 1988, approximately. If he were asked about it today I am not sure that he would go so far as to suggest a date. My own "prediction" is *perhaps* 1998. I emphasize the word *perhaps,* for none of us really knows. It may be in 1988. It may be today or in our generation—that is certainly vague enough. But as I told the man from India, the Lord has not put me on the time committee!

The key piece of the puzzle which has put everything into better perspective fell in place in 1948 when Israel became a nation. Are we living in the time of the end? I believe we definitely are. The Scriptures declare: "Since all these things are to be destroyed in this way, what sort of people ought you to be in holy conduct and godliness, looking for and hastening the coming of the day of God . . . " (2 Pet. 3:11,12).

Our responsibility is not to track down the time or to figure out the precise date when Christ will return. Instead we are to live a life that will glorify God, turn people to Christ, and be a faithful witness to Him. Studying what the Bible has to say will help us fulfill those three holy duties, so let us now examine what the Word says about Jesus and the Middle East.

2
Jesus in Prophecy

For a child will be born to us, a son will be given to us;
And the government will rest on His shoulders;
And His name will be called Wonderful Counselor, Mighty God,
Eternal Father, Prince of Peace.
There will be no end to the increase of His government or of peace.
On the throne of David and over his kingdom,
To establish it and to uphold it with justice and righteousness
From then on and forevermore. . . .

(Is. 9:6,7)

It happened little more than thirty years ago. With the shattering of centuries-old pottery, the world turned its attention to a discovery far greater in value than it dared dream of. Scholars were to call it ''an absolutely incredible find!'' What was it that caused such a stir? And what does it have to do with Jesus in prophecy?

A Bedouin lad named Muhammad adh-Dhib, attempting to flush a stray goat from a cave near the Dead Sea one spring day in 1947, tossed a stone into a small opening of the cave. To his amazement, he heard the distinct shattering of pottery. Perhaps with the hope of finding a treasure of coins he excitedly climbed the barren hillside and squeezed into the cave. There he found a few clay jars, but it was too dark to make out their contents. Besides that, he was frightened. So he returned home and told his uncle what had happened.

The next morning Muhammad and his uncle went to the cave and crawled inside. They discovered twelve pottery jars, one of which contained what looked like a leather scroll wrapped in timeworn linen. This they took to a Bethlehem shoe cobbler, an antique dealer, who gave them a few dollars for the scroll. The man knew enough to turn it over to those who could determine its identity. After being in the possession of Jerusalem's Monastery of St. Mark several months, the scroll and a few other objects from the cave were taken in February 1948 to the acting director of the American Schools of Oriental Research.

There Professor John C. Trever asked permission to examine the scroll, which measured approximately twenty-eight feet in length. For four days and nights Trever photographed the ancient scroll, finding to his delight that it was a copy of the entire book of Isaiah.

Before long the world heard the news. Subsequent excavations at the caves in the vicinity of Qumran yielded more than two hundred scrolls and manuscript fragments. Every Old Testament book, with the exception of Esther, was represented in the remarkable uncovering, including numerous other writings and commentaries. Archaeologists agreed that the site dated to the second century B.C. The ancient manuscripts had been preserved intact for more than two thousand years due to the extremely dry climate of the region.

Until the discovery at Qumran, the oldest known manuscripts of Isaiah were from the ninth century A.D. The discovery of the Dead Sea Scrolls pushed that date back in time a thousand years!

Modernists and liberal scholars who do not believe in the authenticity and inerrancy of the Scriptures have declared for many years that Isaiah could not have written the complete book attributed to him. For one thing, Isaiah, who lived in the seventh century B.C., prophesied events that took place more than a hundred years later, even identifying Cyrus by name, the king who would play a significant role in God's dealings with Israel. Unbelieving scholars have devised intricate explanations for the composition of Isaiah, claiming two, three, or even four authors for the work.

Now, since the discovery of the Dead Sea Scrolls, we see that as early as 150–200 B.C. the book of Isaiah existed complete. While this does not prove that Isaiah was originally written just as we have it today, Professor Charles F. Pfeiffer says, "There is no hint in the Isaiah scrolls (two Isaiah manuscripts were found at Qumran) of a deutero- or trito-Isaiah, to use the language of modern scholarship. The advocates of two or three 'Isaiahs' may suggest that the book was put in its present form prior to the writing of the Qumran manuscripts, but the fact remains that our oldest pre-Christian manuscripts bear witness to the text substantially as we have it in our printed Hebrew Bible." [1]

Scholars continue to study the Dead Sea manuscripts. Josh McDowell says in *Evidence That Demands a Verdict,* "When the facts are known and compared, there is an overwhelming abundance of reasons for believing that the manuscripts we possess are trustworthy." He quotes archaeologist Frederic Kenyon: "The Christian can take the whole Bible in his hand and say without fear of hesitation that he holds in it the true Word of God, handed down without essential loss from generation to generation, throughout the centuries." [2]

Jesus said, "Heaven and earth will pass away, but My words shall not pass away" (Matt. 24:35). Besides Qumran, there have been other significant finds of ancient manuscripts. The discovery, for instance, of New Testament Scriptures stored for centuries in the Monastery of St. Catherine on Mount Sinai received much less attention than its remarkable nature justified. Portions of these and other manuscripts can be viewed in the world's leading museums. On the campus of the Hebrew University in Jerusalem the Dead Sea Scrolls are preserved in the specially built Shrine of the Book.

Found among the manuscripts at Qumran were certain books attributed to the Essenes, Jews who withdrew from the mainstream of Jewish life to form a community. These books speak of a "Teacher of Righteousness" and stress cleansing from sin by baptism. Indeed, once when I visited the archaeological site of Qumran, I counted twenty-seven pools of water in the reconstructed community. The Essenes evidently believed that whenever a person sinned, he must wash away his sins. Knowing human nature, one can imagine how often they had to be baptized!

Early in the 1950s, when the scrolls were just beginning to be examined, critics were convinced that Jesus and John the Baptist were products of Qumran. Yet neither Jesus nor John were recluses, nor were they ever referred to as Essenes. These theories were abandoned as more facts emerged from further study.

Man continues to doubt, but for the open-minded person there is more compelling evidence than even these remarkable ancient manuscripts. We need merely to read the Scriptures and see for ourselves what they say. Usually those unbelievers who attack Scripture have never made a careful study of the Bible for themselves.

The story of Jesus, His life, death, and resurrection is adequately told in the four Gospels. But much of His life was foretold centuries before in prophecy. The Old Testament contains many prophetic passages pointing unquestionably to Jesus, the Messiah who was to come. Realizing that none of these prophecies were written less than four hundred years before Jesus' birth, we know that they are worth our consideration. We now turn to the Scriptures which I consider the highlights of prophecy concerning Jesus.

Prophecies of Jesus in the Historical Books

The first statement in the Bible concerning the Messiah who was to come appears in Genesis.

And I will put enmity
Between you and the woman,
And between your seed and her seed;
He shall bruise you on the head,
And you shall bruise him on the heel
(3:15).

These words are spoken to Satan, the serpent, after he had caused Adam and the woman Eve to sin against God. For centuries the church has understood this text to point to the Seed of the woman, Jesus Christ.

Matthew Poole wrote that "her seed" is "first and principally, the Lord Christ, who with respect to this text, and promise is called, by way of eminency, *the seed,* whose work alone is to break the serpent's head . . . *the head* is the principal instrument both of the serpent's fury and mischief, and of his defense, and the principal seat of the serpent's life, which therefore men chiefly strike at. . . . In the devil this notes his power and authority over men, the strength whereof consists in death, which Christ, the blessed Seed of the woman, overthroweth by taking away *the sting of death, which is sin, and destroying him that had the power of death, that is, the devil.*"[3]

In that garden long ago, God declared that though the devil would be destroyed, he, Satan, would bruise the heel of the Seed of the woman, Christ. At the cross, Christ received these wounds from Satan, but in three days Christ came back to life. Satan's victory was temporal and temporary; Jesus' victory was permanent and eternal.

In Genesis 49:10 we find another intriguing statement. Jacob is near death and he is extending his blessing to each of his twelve sons. To Judah he declares:

The scepter shall not depart from Judah,
Nor the ruler's staff from between his feet,
Until Shiloh comes,
And to him shall be the obedience of the peoples.

Of importance is the declaration that unto this one named Shiloh "the peoples" are to be in obedience. This speaks not of Israel alone, but the nations, a prophecy perfectly in line with what later, fuller revelations tell us of Christ. He is to be "Lord of lords and King of kings."

The traditional understanding of "Shiloh" is "he to whom it (the scepter or kingship) belongs—a Messianic title meaning something like 'the establisher of peace' " says *The New Bible Commentary Revised.*[4] Shiloh is a noun formed from the Hebrew verb "to be quiet, at ease, to enjoy prosperity," quite close in meaning to the greeting *shalom* (*salam* in Arabic), which means peace. When Jesus was born, the announcement from heaven echoed across the Judean hills— "Glory to God in the highest, and on earth peace. . . ." Yes, Genesis 49:10 points far into the future to Jesus.

We find yet still more remarkable prophecies concerning the Messiah in Deuteronomy 18:18,19.

I will raise up a prophet from among their countrymen [brothers] like you, and I will put My words in his mouth, and he shall speak to them all that I command him. And it shall come about that whoever will not listen to My words which he shall speak in My name, I Myself will require it of him.

Peter recognized the messianic meaning of these ancient words of Israel's lawgiver (see Acts 3:22). Jewish scholars have traditionally held that Moses is here foretelling that God will raise up a prophet to serve each generation. But this prophecy promises more than that. It speaks of one to come who was peculiarly to be *like* Moses.

"Moses was a type of Christ both in his life and office," says *The New Bible Commentary Revised.* "Like Jesus his life was spared in infancy, he renounced a royal court to share in the conditions of life of his brethren, and he became a captain of salvation to Israel. He was faithful, full of compassion and love, a powerful intercessor for his people, speaking with God face to face and reflecting the divine glory. Like Christ he was a mighty prophet in word and deed, a revealer of God's will and purpose, a mediator of the covenant and a leader of the people." [5] Yet, as the Israelites did not listen to Moses, so this Scripture announces the judgment of God on "whoever will not listen" to the prophet to come, Christ.

The Psalms

Of the second psalm, Charles Haddon Spurgeon said, "Here is noble proof of the glorious divinity of our Immanuel."

Why are the nations in an uproar,
And the peoples devising a vain thing?
The kings of the earth take their stand,
And the rulers take counsel together
Against the Lord and against His Anointed:
"Let us tear their fetters apart,
And cast away their cords from us!"
He who sits in the heavens laughs,
The Lord scoffs at them.
Then He will speak to them in His anger
And terrify them in His fury:
"But as for Me, I have installed My King
Upon Zion, My holy mountain."
"I will surely tell of the decree of the Lord:
He said to Me, 'Thou art My Son,
Today I have begotten Thee' "
(vv. 1–7).

This treasured psalm of David arises out of its immediate context and finds its true measure in none other than Jesus Christ. The writer of Hebrews twice quoted it (see Heb. 1:5; 5:5) and Paul made reference to it when proving the divinity and eternal sonship of the Lord (see Acts 13:33). Psalm 2 is the first of a number of messianic psalms. The sixteenth is another.

I have set the Lord continually before me;
Because He is at my right hand, I will not be shaken.
Therefore my heart is glad, and my glory rejoices;
My flesh also will dwell securely.
For Thou wilt not abandon my soul to Sheol;
Neither wilt Thou allow Thy Holy One to undergo decay.
Thou wilt make known to me the path of life;
In Thy presence is fulness of joy;
In Thy right hand there are pleasures forever
(vv. 8–11).

Peter, preaching at Pentecost, cited this passage as foretelling the resurrection of Christ (see Acts 2:25–33). And Paul, in the same sermon referred to above, understood David's words to have their primary fulfillment in Christ (see Acts 13:35). As a psalm of David, this poem has fulfilled a vital function by instilling hope and comfort in believers through the ages. But who cannot see in verse 10—"neither wilt Thou allow Thy Holy One to undergo decay''—a reference that uniquely describes the resurrection of our Lord?

Still another of David's psalms, the twenty-second, is almost entirely devoted to a prediction of Christ's sufferings. I have been amazed to find that most Christians are ignorant of this psalm.

My God, my God, why hast Thou forsaken me?
Far from my deliverance are the words of my groaning.
O my God, I cry by day, but Thou dost not answer;
And by night, but I have no rest.
Yet Thou art holy,

O Thou who art enthroned upon the praises of Israel.
In Thee our fathers trusted;
They trusted, and Thou didst deliver them.
To Thee they cried out, and were delivered;
In Thee they trusted, and were not disappointed.
But I am a worm, and not a man,
A reproach of men, and despised by the people.
All who see me sneer at me;
They separate with the lip, they wag the head, saying,
"Commit yourself to the LORD; let Him deliver him;
Let Him rescue him, because He delights in him."
Yet Thou art He who didst bring me forth from the womb;
Thou didst make me trust when upon my mother's breasts.
Upon Thee I was cast from birth;
Thou hast been my God from my mother's womb.
Be not far from me, for trouble is near;
For there is none to help.
Many bulls have surrounded me;
Strong bulls of Bashan have encircled me.
They open wide their mouth at me,
As a ravening and a roaring lion.
I am poured out like water,
And all my bones are out of joint;
My heart is like wax;
It is melted within me.
My strength is dried up like a potsherd,
And my tongue cleaves to my jaws;
And Thou dost lay me in the dust of death.
For dogs have surrounded me;
A band of evildoers has encompassed me;
They pierced my hands and my feet.
I can count all my bones.
They look, they stare at me;
They divide my garments among them,
And for my clothing they cast lots
(vv. 1–18).

Three powerful statements appear in this wonderful psalm
that were fulfilled precisely at the death of Jesus. "My God,

my God, why hast Thou forsaken me?'' were the very words Jesus uttered on the cross. "They pierced my hands and my feet" accurately describes the wounds Jesus suffered when crucified. And finally, "They divide my garments among them, and for my clothing they cast lots" was fulfilled to the letter (see Mark 15:24). A thousand years before Christ these Scriptures were written.

Psalm 69:21 contains an added detail concerning Christ's treatment at Calvary which is as accurate (see Matt. 27:34) as those in Psalm 22. The psalmist there cries: "They also gave me gall for my food,/And for my thirst they gave me vinegar to drink.''

The Prophet Isaiah

Isaiah is called the "prince of prophets" and his book "the fifth Gospel." One of the most extraordinary men who ever lived, his prophetic words carry the same ring of authority as those of the apostles. Is it any surprise that George F. Handel drew so heavily upon Isaiah in composing "The Messiah"? One of the most baffling Scripture verses in Isaiah is this:

Therefore the Lord Himself will give you a sign: Behold, a virgin will be with child and bear a son, and she will call His name Immanuel (7:14).

I suggest that we ought to read this verse "the Lord *Himself* shall give you a sign." God Himself will be a sign. Jesus, who was born of a virgin, is the Lord exactly as John affirms in his gospel (see 1:1,2,14).

For a child will be born to us, a son will be given to us;
And the government will rest on His shoulders;
And His name will be called Wonderful Counselor, Mighty God,
Eternal Father, Prince of Peace.

There will be no end to the increase of His government or of peace,
On the throne of David and over his kingdom,
To establish it and to uphold it with justice and righteousness
From then on and forevermore
(9:6,7).

We are astounded at these words. No man can ever fit or
measure up to this concept except the Son of Man, Jesus of
Nazareth. The titles of esteem and wonder given here for the
virgin-born child clearly point to One who is divine. Jesus was
indeed ''the Mighty God'' (John 10:30), ''the Eternal Father''
(John 14:9), and ''the Prince of Peace'' (Eph. 2:14).

W. A. Criswell lists a number of other messianic
prophecies from Isaiah in the notes to his newly-published
Criswell Study Bible. I will mention only two more in my
discourse here. Certainly the fifty-third chapter is the most
powerful and important; I scarcely need comment on it.

Who has believed our message?
And to whom has the arm of the LORD been revealed?
For He grew up before Him like a tender shoot,
And like a root out of parched ground;
He has no stately form or majesty
That we should look upon Him,
Nor appearance that we should be attracted to Him.
He was despised and forsaken of men,
A man of sorrows, and acquainted with grief;
And like one from whom men hide their face,
He was despised, and we did not esteem Him.
Surely our griefs He Himself bore,
And our sorrows He carried;
Yet we ourselves esteemed Him stricken,
Smitten of God, and afflicted.
But He was pierced through for our transgressions,
He was crushed for our iniquities;
The chastening for our well-being fell upon Him,
And by His scourging we are healed.
All of us like sheep have gone astray,

Each of us has turned to his own way;
But the LORD has caused the iniquity of us all
To fall on Him.
He was oppressed and He was afflicted,
Yet He did not open His mouth;
Like a lamb that is led to slaughter,
And like a sheep that is silent before its shearers,
So He did not open His mouth.
By oppression and judgment He was taken away;
And as for His generation, who considered
That He was cut off out of the land of the living,
For the transgression of my people to whom the stroke was due?
His grave was assigned to be with wicked men,
Yet with a rich man in His death;
Although He had done no violence,
Nor was there any deceit in His mouth.
But the Lord was pleased
To crush Him, putting Him to grief;
If He would render Himself as a guilt offering,
He will see His offspring,
He will prolong His days,
And the good pleasure of the LORD will prosper in His hand.
As a result of the anguish of His soul,
He will see it and be satisfied;
By His knowledge the Righteous One,
My Servant, will justify the many,
As He will bear their iniquities.
Therefore, I will allot Him a portion with the great,
And He will divide the booty with the strong;
Because He poured out Himself to death,
And was numbered with the transgressors;
Yet He Himself bore the sin of many,
And interceded for the transgressors.

Many Jews interpret this immortal Scripture as speaking of the nation of Israel as the suffering servant of Yahweh. But who cannot see in the passage a clear profile of a person—indeed the Messiah? *He* grew up unnoticed and in manhood endured the rejection of His generation. *He* sorrowfully was put to death "for our transgressions." *He* never murmured nor cursed God while He hung upon the cross. *He* compassionately "interceded for the transgressors." *He* died with thieves; yet His body was laid in a rich man's tomb. *He* pleased the Father by laying down His life, thus justifying all who believe in Him. This entire chapter is made plain as one comes to know Jesus.

I rejoice in remembering how Jesus, my Lord, came into the synagogue in Nazareth, the city where I was born and lived until I was fourteen. He was asked to read Scripture and when the scroll was passed to Him he read from Isaiah 61:1–3.

The Spirit of the Lord GOD is upon me,
Because the LORD has anointed me
To bring good news to the afflicted;
He has sent me to bind up the brokenhearted,
To proclaim liberty to captives,
And freedom to prisoners;
To proclaim the favorable year of the LORD,
And the day of vengeance of our God;
To comfort all who mourn,
To grant those who mourn in Zion,
Giving them a garland instead of ashes,
The oil of gladness instead of mourning,
The mantle of praise instead of a spirit of fainting.
So they will be called oaks of righteousness,
The planting of the LORD, that He may be glorified.

Seven centuries passed after Isaiah spoke those words. Then Jesus appeared in the Nazareth Sabbath service, read the passage, and declared: "Today this Scripture has been fulfilled in your hearing" (Luke 4:21).

It is worth noting that at Nazareth He did not quote the entire passage. According to Luke, He stopped with "the favorable year of the Lord," indicating that His mission on earth was then to preach the good news of the kingdom and to release those who are spiritually enslaved by Satan. The further words concerning ''the day of vengeance'' are yet to be fulfilled at His second coming.

The Minor Prophets

The Bible verses quoted thus far are convincing proof that God spoke through His prophets foretelling the coming of the Messiah. Let us now look at four or five quotations from those shorter books popularly known as ''minor prophets.''

In the book of Micah, the birthplace of the coming Messiah was predicted.

But as for you, Bethlehem Ephrathah,
Too little to be among the clans of Judah,
From you One will go forth for Me to be ruler in Israel.
His goings forth are from long ago,
From the days of eternity (5:2).

Since Micah lived in the time of King Hezekiah, he made this prophecy some eight centuries before Christ. Luke recorded its fulfillment in his documentary/biography of Jesus. The wise men of the East were able to find their way to the newborn King by consulting Herod's rabbi (see Matt. 2:1–9).

In approximately 520 B.C. Zechariah predicted unthinkable details of the plot and betrayal of Jesus.

And I said to them, ''If it is good in your sight, give me my wages; but if not, never mind!'' So they weighed out thirty shekels of silver as my wages. Then the Lord said to me, ''Throw it to the potter, that magnificent price at which I was valued by them.'' So I took the thirty shekels of silver and threw them to the potter in the house of the LORD (11:12,13).

What Zechariah said came to pass. Judas betrayed Jesus for thirty pieces of silver and then cast the money before the priests in the house of the Lord. They in turn purchased the potter's field with the "blood money" and set it apart for a burying place for strangers (see Matt. 27:7).

The doctrine of the Trinity, faintly foreshadowed in the Old Testament, comes to its fullest expression in the New Testament. But Zechariah's pen, divinely inspired, foretold the sonship of the Messiah in this passage, as well as revealing the concept of the Father and the Spirit:

And I will pour out on the house of David and on the inhabitants of Jerusalem, the Spirit of grace and of supplication, so that they will look on Me whom they have pierced; and they will mourn for Him, as one mourns for an only son, and they will weep bitterly over Him, like the bitter weeping over a first-born (12:10).

This mysterious passage speaks of both the first and second advents of our Lord. "So that they will look on Me whom they have pierced" indicates Jesus' first coming. The verse also predicts that Israel will repent of their rejection of their Messiah and "weep bitterly over Him" as they realize He is the Father's "only son." Zechariah thus sees beyond the first coming to the future when the Jews have been gathered again in the land. This returning to Jerusalem occurred in 1967, and now we wait patiently for the time when Jews will believe in the Lord Jesus Christ. I am convinced it can happen in our lifetime. Beyond any doubt, though, it will happen.

In the closing book of the Old Testament, God announces:

Behold, I am going to send My messenger, and he will clear the way before Me. And the Lord, whom you seek, will suddenly come to His temple; and the messenger of the covenant, in whom you delight, behold, He is coming," says the LORD of hosts (Mal. 3:1).

A related passage is found in the final chapter:

Behold, I am going to send you Elijah the prophet before the coming of the great and terrible day of the LORD (4:5).

Mark opens his gospel with the earlier statement from Malachi, linking Jesus with the pronouncement concerning the Lord's coming suddenly to His temple. The messenger in Malachi is identified as Elijah in chapter four, and in the Gospels we learn from Jesus that John the Baptist is the one intended. The statement concerning the ''Elijah'' is in the last book of the Old Testament. To the very end, the Old Testament Scriptures were pointing to the Messiah.

3

Signs of the Return— Fulfilled

And when He had spoken these things, while they watched, He was taken up, and a cloud received Him out of their sight. And while they looked steadfastly toward heaven as He went up, behold, two men stood by them in white apparel, who also said, "Men of Galilee, why do you stand gazing up into heaven? This same Jesus, who was taken up from you into heaven, will so come in like manner as you have seen Him go into heaven."

(Acts 1:9–11 NKJB–NT)

Every page of the Bible reflects divine inspiration. From Genesis to Revelation the story of redemption unfolds. There is no book like the Bible anywhere, so full of God's love as found in law and history, narrative and poetry—and prophecy. Of the sixty-six books in the Bible, seventeen in the Old Testament and one in the New Testament are devoted almost exclusively to foretelling the message of God.

We have seen how the Old Testament Scriptures spoke in detail about the first coming of Jesus, to redeem man from sin. The prophets were God's messengers, hurling fiery warnings against the evils of their age, urging people to flee the wrath to come. They foretold the movements of men and nations, often

25

centuries before the event. Only God could have known of these things. The fact that history records their fulfillment, exactly and completely, is the seal of authenticity of the whole Bible.

Modern day seers and fortune-tellers would have us believe they can be depended on, though actually they prove to be wrong half of the time. They would never measure up to God's absolute standards for dependability—"When a prophet speaks in the name of the LORD, if the thing does not come about or come true, that is the thing which the LORD has not spoken. The prophet has spoken it presumptuously; you shall not be afraid of him" (Deut. 18:22). Biblical prophecy is the indestructible fortress that no enemy hosts have been able to overcome.

Still, many Christians today—I would say the majority—avoid prophecy and its study as if it were a malignant disease. Three reasons for this attitude are prominent:

1. Some shy away from the mystery of prophecy, feeling that nothing prophetic can be understood with any degree of certainty. Therefore, they neither heed its message nor claim its blessings.

2. Others go along with the unbelieving world, denying that anything can be true which cannot be explained rationally or verified scientifically. Most theologians today question the supernatural and thus do not take prophecy seriously.

3. Still others—I do not know how many—shy away from the subject because certain teachers have set dates for the Second Coming and the end of the world. A few extremists have made many Christians leery of the whole subject. In the preface to his book *Egypt and Israel: Coming Together?* the noted Bible teacher Wilbur M. Smith calls date setting a "wretched business" and says that "though condemned repeatedly by the failure of these chronological schemes" there are always those "engaged in such folly." [1]

The believer has much to gain from acknowledging

prophecy. Jesus and His apostles emphasized the importance of prophecy and made use of it time and again. If the Old Testament foretold the coming of the Messiah in detail, the New Testament speaks of His coming again even more. For every verse dealing with the First Advent there are three describing His Second Advent.

Peter wrote, "For no prophecy was ever made by an act of human will, but men moved by the Holy Spirit spoke from God" (2 Pet. 1:21). Concerning the prophetic word he said we ought to pay attention, "as to a lamp shining in a dark place, until the day dawns and the morning star arises in your hearts" (2 Pet. 1:19). Peter himself preached the first gospel sermon from the prophecies of Joel and David which, as he preached, were being fulfilled. Other Christian leaders also espoused the role of prophecy. Philip read from the prophet Isaiah and preached to the Ethiopian (see Acts 8:29–35; Is. 53:7,8). Paul declared that the office of prophet in the church was second in importance only to that of the apostle (see Eph. 4:11).

Before examining the prophecies concerning Jesus' second coming let us review how some of the Old Testament prophecies have been fulfilled.

Great Events Were Foretold

Through Noah, God warned the ancient world of the Flood.

By faith Noah, being warned by God about things not yet seen, in reverence prepared an ark for the salvation of his household, by which he condemned the world, and became an heir of the righteousness which is according to faith (Heb. 11:7).

Undaunted, Noah preached for an estimated 120 years though no one heeded him. By modern standards, Noah would be considered a failure. But he was faithful to what God told him to do, and faithfulness is success in God's eyes.

God reasoned concerning the judgment He would send upon Sodom and Gomorrah, "Shall I hide from Abraham what I am about to do?" (Gen. 18:17). Instead, before the event He told Abraham that the two wicked cities would be destroyed. Anyone who has ever witnessed the ruins of Pompeii can appreciate something of the destruction of Sodom and Gomorrah. A few years ago I saw the ruins of Pompeii and for the first time realized why the city was buried in lava and ashes. It was a place of unbelievable moral decadence.

Much later in history God had this to say concerning the powerful nation of Babylon:

"And this whole land shall be a desolation and a horror, and these nations shall serve the king of Babylon seventy years. Then it will be when seventy years are completed I will punish the king of Babylon and that nation," declares the LORD, "for their iniquity, and the land of the Chaldeans; and I will make it an everlasting desolation" (Jer. 25:11,12).

The prophet Jeremiah predicted that Israel would be held captive in Babylon for seventy years, after which Israel would return to Jerusalem. Cyrus, King of Persia, was only doing his appointed task when in 539 B.C., exactly seventy years later, he proclaimed the return of the Jews to their homeland.

In the sixth century B.C. the prophet Obadiah foretold the destruction of the city of Petra, the ancient stronghold of Esau's descendants (see vv. 2–4,8). This city once accommodated one hundred thousand people and thought its defenses invincible. Today the only people in this city are tourists. A four-hour drive south from Amman, Petra is beautiful but deserted—a city judged by God and forgotten by civilization. Similar prophecies were voiced concerning Babylon, Sidon, Tyre, and Nineveh.

Time after time Israel saw the Word of the Lord fulfilled. Still they would not believe. Why should they have thought it so incredible that the Son of God would be born of a virgin (see

Is. 7:14) when the supernatural had always been a part of their very existence? Nothing is too hard for the almighty God of the cosmos. When Christ came the first time He found only a few people waiting for His coming—Anna and Simeon at the Jerusalem Temple, the wise men from the East, and a few other devout people. Is it any wonder today that so few are looking for Him to return? I am not at all surprised that many religious leaders and biblical scholars are unconcerned and indifferent about His coming. That is the way it was when Jesus first came.

Inasmuch as His first coming was according to prophecy and took place as foretold, we can expect the prophecies of His second coming also to be fulfilled in a literal way. Numerous signs have been given that are to be fulfilled. Indeed, ninety percent of what is foretold as taking place before the return of Christ has already been fulfilled. Every day brings us closer to our Ultimate Hope—Christ's return.

The State of Israel

When I drive home from the airport after a trip, I know that I am nearly home when I begin to recognize familiar landmarks in the neighborhood. When I turn onto the street where our family lives and see the sights I've grown accustomed to, I know that I will be home momentarily. So it is with Christ's coming. He gave us signs and said that when we see these things coming to pass we will know that the return of the Son of Man is near. One sign that He gave is the return of Israel to their ancient homeland.

The prophet Zechariah said there would come a time when the Jews would return to their land.

Thus says the LORD of hosts, "Behold, I am going to save My people from the land of the east and from the land of the west; and I will bring them back, and they will live in the midst of Jerusalem, and they will be My people and I will be their God in truth and righteousness'' (Zech. 8:7,8).

This is an unequivocal promise that the Jews would return to ancient Palestine and become a nation. On May 15, 1948, this was fulfilled. But throughout this century the Jewish people have been returning to Palestine. Approximately 52,000 Jews inhabited Palestine in 1900. The latest figures now show that 3.2 million Jews are living within the borders of Israel. A timetable for the creation of the nation of Israel would look like this:

1917   Lord Balfour, Britain's foreign secretary, approves a plan for a ''national home'' for the Jewish people in Palestine. The U.S. endorses the plan, known as the Balfour Declaration.

1923   Britain is given control over Palestine by the League of Nations and promises the Jews ''a national home'' in Palestine.

1947   The United Nations adopts a plan to partition Palestine.

1948   On May 15 the Jews in Palestine declare the creation of the independent nation Israel. Immediately war breaks out with five Arab nations. On June 1, Israel and the Arab nations accept a UN resolution for a truce in Palestine.

1967   The Six Day War begins on June 4. Israel is attacked but swiftly destroys much of the enemy's fighting capacity and gains extensive territory, chiefly Jerusalem. For the first time it has possession of the entire city of Jerusalem as well as the West Bank of the Jordan River, formerly Jordanian territory, and the Gaza Strip, formerly held by Egypt.

1973   On Yom Kippur, the Jewish Day of Atonement, Egypt and Syria launch a powerful attack on Israel, almost overwhelming the unsuspecting nation.

1977   In March, Israel raids Palestinian commando positions in southern Lebanon. In November, President Anwar el-Sadat of Egypt makes his historic visit to Jerusalem.

1978   On September 20 the Camp David peace accords are signed by President Jimmy Carter of the United States, President Sadat of Egypt, and Prime Minister Menachem Begin of Israel.

1979   On March 26, a peace treaty between Egypt and Israel is signed at the White House; the U.S. is a full partner in the agreement.

As a lad growing up in Nazareth in 1948, I heard much about how our neighboring Arab states were going to help us keep Palestine for the Arabs. At the outset of the war that year, the Arab forces seemed to have the upper hand. Then Israel showed surprising strength. At the time of the United Nations' intervention which brought an uneasy truce, my hometown of Nazareth was already in Israeli hands. My father and cousin were dead; my mother, sister, brother, and I were among 650,000 Arab refugees without a home. We fled on camelback across the border into Jordan, hoping to return in a short while. Only in 1968, twenty years later, did I go back to my hometown. That year I led my first tour group from America to the Holy Land and the highlight for me, of course, was when the tour bus brought us to Nazareth. There I was reunited with my aged grandmother who lived on the outskirts of the town, and I saw the house my father had built, where I had lived until the war. The trees that grace the landscape were much larger and the place looked smaller through my adult eyes, but most everything else was the same.

Even though I grew up in Palestine, I never imagined there might be a deeper meaning to the crises in the Middle East until I began to see the amazing correlation of these events with biblical prophecies. Even as far back as Jeremiah's time, it was prophesied that the Jews would once again use their ancient language in this land. ''Thus saith the LORD of hosts, the God of Israel; As yet they shall use this speech in the land of Judah and in the cities thereof, when I shall bring again their captivity . . .'' (Jer. 31:23 KJV). Today, in fulfillment of this prophecy of the seventh century B.C., Hebrew is the official language of Israel. It had been virtually a dead language for twenty-four hundred years. Fantastic, but true.

In 1980 another incredible incident occurred, similar to the revival of Hebrew as a language. Israel introduced a ''new'' currency, replacing the lira with the shekel, Israel's form of currency *two millennia ago.*

Yet another prophecy concerning the state of Israel demands our notice. Ezekiel prophesied that the desolate land will become like the Garden of Eden.

And the desolate land will be cultivated instead of being a desolation in the sight of everyone who passed by. And they will say, ''This desolate land has become like the garden of Eden; and the waste, desolate, and ruined cities are fortified and inhabited'' (36:34,35).

Every year I lead a tour group to the Middle East and on every visit I am impressed with the blossoming of the land. Many of the people taking the tours have seen my beautiful color film, ''Where Jesus Walked,'' and expect the beauty they see. ''The Israelis have nearly tripled their total cropland since 1948,'' says the *World Book Encyclopedia,* ''by draining swamps, expanding irrigation and ending soil erosion. Fruits and vegetables and flowers are growing in abundance and whole forests have been replanted.'' [2]

Jerusalem

Jesus said, according to Luke's gospel, that the city of Jerusalem would be ''trodden down'' until the times of the Gentiles are fulfilled (see Luke 21:24). The ''times of the Gentiles'' should be dated from A.D. 70 when Jerusalem was destroyed by Roman armies. At that time, though the apostles continued to evangelize the Jews, God began giving the salvation to non-Jews. The door of the gospel swung wide open to the Gentiles and before long the number of Gentile Christians far outnumbered that of Jewish Christians. Dispensationalists call this the "age of grace," a time of presenting the gospel to all nations. It continues to our day. But the Six-Day War aroused serious expectations among students of the Bible.

For the first time in almost two thousand years, Israel gained possession of the entire city of Jerusalem. Until then, Jews were cut off from Old Jerusalem where the Temple Mount is located. "The Israelis will never relinquish their control of it," declared the Israeli war hero, Moshe Dayan. To the consternation of their surrounding Arab neighbors, Israel has proceeded with plans to make Jerusalem a permanent Jewish city. Does this signal that the "times of the Gentiles" are near an end? Many Christian teachers think it does. God seems to be drawing His people into the land so that He may deal with them as a people and so that the Messiah may return to the city and rule.

But meanwhile Israel threatens to push its advantage too far. With the announcement in July 1980 by the Knesset that Israel was formally annexing Jerusalem, Arab nations countered with a threat of *jihad* (holy war). Saudi Arabia's Crown Prince Fahd proposed an Islamic retaliation; and at a meeting in Morocco in September 1980 foreign ministers of the world's Islamic nations laid plans for a possible holy war. Tunisia's Habib Chatti, secretary general of the conference, said the Islamic countries "envisaged the *jihad* for the liberation of Jerusalem first of all as a worldwide political, diplomatic and economic 'harassment' of Israel and its allies, culminating in military action only if all else failed." [3] President Carter's envoy to the Middle East, Sol Linowitz, urged Prime Minister Begin not to relocate his office in the annexed Arab sector of Jerusalem and for a time the tension eased.

Who is to say when the Arabs might carry out their threats? A dozen years ago Bible teacher Daniel Fuchs of the American Board of Missions to the Jews, in pondering the possibility of the Jews rebuilding the temple in Jerusalem, said such an action "could result in the War of Armageddon." [4]

Zechariah 14:1–3 says:

Behold, a day is coming for the LORD when the spoil taken from you will be divided among you. For I will gather all the nations against Jerusalem to battle, and the city will be captured, the houses plundered, the women ravished, and half of the city exiled, but the rest of the people will not be cut off from the city. Then the LORD will go forth and fight against those nations, as when He fights on a day of battle."

Surely peace is elusive in the lands of the Bible. Arabs and Jews will never be reconciled except by the cross of Jesus and His redeeming love. As events take place in Jerusalem we believe they signal the imminent return of the Messiah.

Knowledge on the Increase

The prophet Daniel said that in the last times ". . . many shall run to and fro, and knowledge shall be increased" (12:4 KJV). Many scholars have interpreted that to mean that as the last days come, people will search everywhere (except in the Scriptures) to find the Messiah or to discover some trace of solid information about the future. Another interpretation is possible. "Many shall run to and fro" could have reference to the incredible strides in transportation that man has made in the twentieth century. We think nothing these days of flying a jet airplane halfway around the world or even of sending spaceships to the moon. But our great-grandparents would have considered such travel the mad imaginings of a dreamer.

Or consider the prophecy that "knowledge will increase." Could this anticipate the tremendous information explosion in the latter half of the twentieth century? I am told that one-half of all the world's scientific knowledge has been acquired in the last sixteen years. Something like 95 percent of all the scientists who ever lived are alive today, stimulating in every field a great quest for knowledge. Mathematics, medicine, marketing, astronomy, biology, farming, archaeology, space technology, electronic communications—all of these fields are constantly transformed because of recent advancements and brilliant discoveries. If this prophecy does speak of travel and knowledge in this sense, then no other time in man's history so well meets the criteria for fulfillment as the present age. Note, however, the Scripture claims knowledge, not *wisdom,* is to increase before the end.

Social, Spiritual, and Moral Decline

We are now a world plagued by material and physical needs, enmeshed in the turmoil of political intrigue and pride. Our times are much like the days of Noah.

For as in those days which were before the flood they were eating and drinking, they were marrying and giving in marriage, until the day that Noah entered the ark, and they did not understand until the flood came and took them all away, so shall the coming of the Son of Man be (Matt. 24:38,39).

In his recent book, *Listen, America!,* Jerry Falwell documents the alarming degree of decadence in America. Falwell writes:

In the past 10 years violent crimes have increased 173 per cent in America. Murder is up 129 per cent. Aggravated assault is up 139 per cent. . . . Drug addiction and alcoholism are in pandemic proportions. . . . there are more than 9 million alcoholics in the United States. . . . We have teen-agers who are experimenting with sex in the most vile form, while teen-age pregnancies, incest, and sexual child abuse are rampant problems. Gonorrhea is now contracted by more than 2 million Americans each year. . . . A thriving new industry floods into the nation's homes through pornographic literature and television programs. . . . America's homes are in trouble.

America's homes are the stabilizing factors in our society, yet the family is disintegrating at an alarming rate. Nearly 1 out of 2 marriages is ending in divorce. . . . *Each day* more than 4,000 unborn babies are destroyed by abortion. . . . Sin has permeated our land.[5]

I was shocked beyond belief in the summer of 1980 upon reading that a man and his wife from Arkansas sought to trade in their little infant daughter for a new car. The auto dealer in New Jersey where the couple had traveled was incensed at their proposition, but went along with it in order to turn them over to the police.

We cannot escape. The mad pursuit of pleasure, materialism, and sex has brought down other great world powers before America. Since these corrupting practices are now no longer limited to a single nation or culture but are worldwide, anyone can predict the consequences that await our world.

Every day newspapers describe the latest incidences of man's inhumanity to man. In every realm, especially among the younger generation, men and women are rebelling against authority. You may be surprised to know that even this spiritual and moral decay was foretold for the latter days:

But realize this, that in the last days difficult times will come. For men will be lovers of self, lovers of money, boastful, arrogant, revilers, disobedient to parents, ungrateful, unholy, unloving, irreconcilable, malicious gossips, without self-control, brutal, haters of good, treacherous, reckless, conceited, lovers of pleasure rather than lovers of God; holding to a form of godliness, although they have denied its power; and avoid such men as these (2 Tim. 3:1–5).

Paul concluded his first letter to the Corinthian church with the Aramaic expression "Maranatha." It means "the Lord comes" or "the Lord is returning." As we see all about us the signs of our Lord's coming already fulfilled, let us echo what John declared—"even so, come, Lord Jesus!"

4

Signs of the Return — Being Fulfilled

But concerning the times and the seasons, brethren, you have no need that I write to you. For you yourselves know perfectly that the day of the Lord so comes as a thief in the night. For when they say, "Peace and safety!" then sudden destruction comes on them, as labor pains on a pregnant woman. And they shall not escape. But you, brethren, are not in darkness, that this Day should overtake you as a thief. You are all sons of light and sons of the day. We are not of the night nor of darkness. Therefore let us not sleep, as others do, but let us watch and be sober.

(1 Thess. 5:1–6 NKJB–NT)

As we have seen, the presence of three million Jews in their homeland and the existence of the state of Israel are of themselves clear indications that we are near the time of Christ's return. Someone has said that Israel is God's "timepiece" and that if we would rightly understand history, we should watch Israel. I believe it. Israel's rebirth signals His soon return.

Since 1967 I have made more than a dozen trips to the Holy Land, leading groups of Christian pilgrims through the land of the Bible. There we see firsthand the immense achievements in Israel. Though beset by severe inflation, Israel is constructing buildings on a grand scale and opening more and more acreage for agriculture. The land is in ". . . blossom as the rose" (Is. 35:1 KJV). Simultaneously international teams of archaeologists continue their digs, and what they are finding serves to remind the present generation of Israel's rich past.

The Temple

On June 16, 1977, an article appeared in the *Mobile* (Ala.) *Press* and in numerous other papers across America and read as follows.

A grandiose plan to turn the Wailing Wall area in the old city of Jerusalem into a great plaza and synagogue for hundreds of thousands of Jewish worshipers has been approved by a government-appointed committee and presented to Justice Minister Haim Zadok.

The minister said the plan would be passed on to the incoming Likud government for consideration.

If carried out, the plan would transform the precincts within the old walls of the city into an impressive monumental plaza rivaling that of St. Peter's in Rome or the one facing the Moslem shrine of the Dome of the Rock just north of the Wailing Wall.

The ambitious plan elaborated by architect Moshe Safti, the conceiver of the "habitat" structures, provides for the landscaping of the present area of the holiest Jewish shrine. It contains the remains of the western wall of King Herod's Biblical temple of Jerusalem built some 2,000 years ago and destroyed by the Roman legions of Titus when they captured Jerusalem in 70 A.D.

The Safti plan calls for the lowering of the existing prayer area in front of the Wailing Wall. This would permit reaching the original Herodian level and reveal a few more rows of the great granite square blocks that make up the wall and before which Jews have been praying for 2,000 years, lamenting the loss of Jerusalem.

The lowered area would be turned into a synagogue and open only to those taking part in services.

Rising from the foot of the Wall to the south would be a series of terraces reaching the ancient Jewish quarter. These terraces would have access to the old city walls and gates.

There are no Arab holy sites within the Wailing Wall area and apparently no new Arab property would be affected as far as the preliminary plans are known.

Some old Arab houses that used to face the Wailing Wall when the Israelis entered the old city in 1967 were razed in the very first weeks of Israeli control. Their Arab residents were provided with other housing. . . .[1]

This story is of interest to students of the Bible for it seems to lend credence to a most important possibility—the building of a new temple. The daily prayer of the Orthodox Jew is, ''May it be Thy will that the temple be speedily rebuilt in our days.'' Ever since Israel regained control of Old Jerusalem, speculation has grown about a new temple. While neither Israel's government nor its Orthodox community has ever announced that it intends to build a new temple (Orthodox Jews believe the Messiah will rebuild the temple when He comes), a more important question must be satisfactorily answered beforehand: *Exactly where was the original temple built?* No site on earth is more dear to the Jew than the temple, which contained the Holy of Holies where God covenanted to meet His people. It was on the mercy seat, the golden covering of the ark of the covenant, that the high priest sprinkled the blood offering on the Day of Atonement. Throughout its history, until the Herodian temple was destroyed in A.D. 70, this sanctuary was the focal point of Jewish worship. It would be unthinkable for another temple to be built anywhere but on that same historic site.

For centuries it has been assumed that the massive rock beneath the Dome of the Rock (also called the Mosque of Omar, built in A.D. 691) was the foundation stone on which the ark of the covenant rested. Thus, any attempt to build a new temple was ruled out. Muslim devotion to this mosque is as great as would be the Jewish devotion to a new temple. Yet, because the entire Temple Mount is under the jurisdiction of the Supreme Muslim Council in Old Jerusalem, no archaeological explorations are allowed even though Israel has taken control of the whole city. So, the historic site of the temple remains a mystery.

On April 6, 1980, the international edition of the *Jerusalem Post* carried a two-page spread devoted to the theory of an Orthodox physicist that the ancient temple was built on a different site. Even more exciting, according to his theory the ancient temple site is not on the same ground as the Dome of the Rock. He claims a new temple could be erected without touching the Dome.

Dr. Asher Kaufman, an English scientist who immigrated with his family to Palestine in 1959, took a year's sabbatical from his duties at the Hebrew University to try to determine the location of the original temple. When asked why he was so interested in locating the temple site, he answers, "I don't know." His research took him to the ancient writings (called *Middot*), dating to the period of the second temple (Herod's temple was an elaborate expansion of Zerubbabel's temple; hence scholars refer to it also as the second temple). He made studious use of aerial photographs of Jerusalem, especially those made by German aviators in 1918. And he continued to read the Old Testament Scriptures. According to the *Jerusalem Post* article, Dr. Kaufman came to understand a key part of the puzzle while reading a portion of Ezekiel.

Since no Orthodox Jew is allowed to tread upon the Temple Mount for fear one might inadvertently walk upon the Holy of Holies, it seemed Dr. Kaufman was forbidden to explore the possible site first-hand. However, on looking into the matter, he discovered that as a non-priest he could explore the area if he were considered cleaning, repairing, or rebuilding the temple. The latter suited his conscience and he was able to gain entrance, though he insists the ''rebuilding'' is for him purely theoretical.

What Dr. Kaufman found convinced him that the smaller Dome of the Spirits (see photo section) on the Temple Mount was the location of the Holy of Holies. In the spring issue of *Christian News from Israel* (1979) Dr. Kaufman published his findings, including an outline superimposed over a drawing of the main features of the Temple Mount as it is today. The outline is Dr. Kaufman's studied opinion of how the second temple was laid out and where its walls stood. He concludes that article reverently:

The picture of the Second Temple that has been pieced together from archaeological and other sources is no longer a mere sketch; rather it approaches the architectural plan of an actual building. And, most importantly, it would appear that Divine Providence has ensured that no major structure occupy the actual site of the Temple. . . . the magnificent Dome of the Rock, stands south of the Temple site. Does this fact, together with the Jewish return to the Land, augur the Latter Days prophesied by Isaiah (56:7): ''And I shall bring them to My holy mountain, . . . for My house shall be called a house of prayer for all peoples''?[2]

I hasten again to say that I know of no plan to construct a temple at this spot. To do so would undoubtedly enrage Muslims and galvanize them to fulfill their threats of a holy war.

Yet reports surface that indicate that the present generation is making preparations for a temple. An unconfirmed story says that as of Hanukkah 1978 some *Hasidim* (ultra-religious Jews) opened a school to train young students in the laws of sacrifice. It is said that in order to be admitted these youths must be able to trace their ancestry to Aaron. Basic to the observance of the temple ritual and sacrificial system is a knowledge of biblical weights and measures. Thanks to archaeological research, these facts are now known.

Orthodox Jews and premillennial Christians have always believed one thing in common—that a temple would be erected on the site of Solomon's temple. They come to this conclusion because they both accept the Scriptures literally. Daniel's prophecy of the seventieth week, which we shall discuss later, says that the Antichrist will interrupt temple worship when he bursts forth. Paul also declares that the Antichrist will occupy the temple (see 2 Thess. 2:4). How is the temple to be occupied, it is argued, unless a third temple is built? I believe a temple of national importance is to be built soon to provide such a stage before the return of our Lord. Jerusalem is getting ready to build it too, as Revelation 11:1,2 prophesied years ago:

. . ."Rise and measure the temple of God, and the altar, and those who worship in it. And leave out the court which is outside the temple, and do not measure it, for it has been given to the nations. . . ."

Thus it appears that the Dome of the Rock with its magnificent beauty, ancient history, and remarkable position as a world famous monument will neither be dismantled nor destroyed to make room for the new temple.

In 1976 Israeli archaeologists announced their discovery of the secret underground stairway which the high priest used for his annual appearance at the holy place. The tremendous crowds and the fear of being defiled dictated his use of the passage to go into God's presence. We can go underground today to see the excavations near the Wailing Wall.

Is it possible that the ark of the covenant will be found before the temple is finished? No temple would become the temple without the ark. The temple contained the ark, the candlestick, the table of shewbread, the altar of incense, the altar of sacrifice, the laver, and the golden-covered mercy seat on which rested the two cherubim. All of these objects can be reconstructed except the ark. It can never be replaced since it contained the tablets of the Ten Commandments and the rod of Aaron.

One may remember John's vision, recorded in Revelation 11:19, in which he tells of seeing the ark in heaven. But that is not the ark the children of Israel carried with them. Moses was told to build the various elements for the tabernacle "according to all that I [God] am going to show you, as the pattern . . ." (Ex. 25:9). The ark constructed in the wilderness and later placed in the temple was modeled after the true ark in heaven.

A few years ago a friend of mine called me from the Holy Land and said he was joining a search party looking for the ancient ark. Dr. Kaufman believes it was buried in the chamber next to the Court of the Women on the temple grounds. It seems like idle talk to speak of finding the ark, but if it should be discovered, nothing would bring more devotion and revival to Israel. The entire world would be stirred to seek God. Furthermore, in January 1982 a brief news report announced that the ark was found in a secret cavern on the huge mountain of Nebo in Jordan. Jewish documents have held for a long time that Jeremiah the prophet secretly carried the ark and hid it in Mount Nebo before the fall of Jerusalem.

The Golden Gate

Jerusalem is a city of gates, and one of these gates has been singled out for special service in the days of the "prince," the Messiah. Ezekiel said of this gate:

Then He brought me back by the way of the outer gate of the sanctuary, which faces the east; and it was shut. And the LORD said to me, "This gate shall be shut; it shall not be opened, and no one shall enter by it, for the LORD God of Israel has entered by it; therefore it shall be shut. As for the prince, He shall sit in it as prince to eat bread before the LORD; he shall enter by way of the porch of the gate, and shall go out by the same way'' (44:1–3).

The ''outer gate of the sanctuary, which faces the east'' is the one known variously as the Eastern Gate or the Golden Gate. In Arabic it is called *Bab ed Dahariyeh,* the Eternal Gate. A fascinating history is associated with this gate, a full account of which can be found in G. Frederick Owen's *Jerusalem.*[3] The Eastern Gate (see photo section) faces the Mount of Olives and it would be the entrance to the city which our Lord used when he rode into Jerusalem on a colt as the people waved palm branches and shouted, ''Hosanna, blessed is he who comes in the name of the Lord.''

The prophecy above declares that ''the Lord God of Israel'' would enter the gate and then it would be shut until a time in the future when the prince ''shall enter by way of it.'' This gate has been walled up since Jerusalem fell into the hands of the Muslims, with the brief exception of the period A.D. 1102–1187 when Christians liberated the city during the Crusades. Kaiser Wilhelm of Germany reportedly intended to make his ceremonial entry into the city in 1898 through this historic gate, but for some reason chose an entrance on the opposite side of the city. When Jordan attempted to open it, they lost control of Jerusalem in 1967. Israel, too, may lose the city should it decide to reopen the Golden Gate.

The Mount of Olives

When Jesus entered Jerusalem by the Golden Gate on Palm Sunday, He came by way of the Mount of Olives. Matthew, in recording this event in 21:1–10, quotes a prophecy from Zechariah (9:9) fulfilled on that day. Another of Zechariah's prophetic utterances is yet to be fulfilled at Christ's return.

And in that day His feet will stand on the Mount of Olives, which is in front of Jerusalem on the east; and the Mount of Olives will be split in its middle from east to west by a very large valley, so that half of the mountain will move toward the north and the other half toward the south (14:4).

Jesus ascended to glory from the Mount of Olives and we expect Him to return and set foot on the Mount of Olives. This Scripture teaches that geographical changes will take place when He does. Perhaps it will be an earthquake which splits the mountain since earthquakes are common in that region. Recently, for instance, the owners of a large hotel chain canceled their plans to build on the Mount of Olives because engineers warned them that the area is unstable. One can stand on the Temple Mount, near the Eastern Wall, and see a depression in the mountain which makes it look like two humps of a camel. Perhaps the splitting has already begun, awaiting even a minor earthquake for the final rending of the mountain.

Apparently as a result of the miracle foretold in 14:4, another geographical change will take place, as foretold in Zechariah 14:8.

And it will come about in that day that living waters will flow out of Jerusalem, half of them toward the eastern sea and the other half toward the western sea; it will be in summer as well as in winter.

Undoubtedly God will accomplish this by supernatural intervention. Yet I was intrigued a year ago to hear a radio report from Israel bearing directly on this prophecy. A group of Israeli engineers presented a plan for a canal connecting the Dead Sea with the Mediterranean Sea. Evidently the idea was considered feasible since the August 25, 1980 Washington *Post* wire service carried the announcement "Israel Approves Plan to Build Canal Through the Gaza Strip." The story claimed that Israel's cabinet had "approved a plan to construct a 61-mile long canal from the Mediterranean Sea to the Dead

Sea to provide hydroelectric power and raise the level of the Dead Sea.'' [4] The construction would raise the waters of the Dead Sea an estimated fifty-six feet, facilitating the mining of potash in the sea. Such a canal might also provide Israel and Jordan with an inland waterway for maritime shipping.

Zechariah's prophecy could be interpreted in a spiritual sense, meaning that Jerusalem (or Israel) will in the latter days be as a fountain of living waters to the nations of the world, bringing spiritual life to all. But could it not also be literally fulfilled? This canal is expected to be at least ten years in the digging; and though it appears now that there is no plan for its course to come near the city of Jerusalem, one wonders if within a few decades an earthquake might create a crevice which would cause the Mediterranean to flow into the Jordan Valley. If that happens, the entire valley could be flooded, with water reaching halfway from Jericho to Jerusalem. Since Jerusalem is 2000 feet above sea level and the Dead Sea is approximately 1,300 feet below, it would take only a few days to accomplish such a miracle!

The Search for Peace

A further sign for which we are to watch—a sign that is being fulfilled right before our eyes—is the worldwide hunger for peace. In speaking of the return of Christ, Paul said, ''For when they say, 'Peace and safety!' then sudden destruction comes on them, as labor pains on a pregnant woman. And they shall not escape'' (1 Thess. 5:3 NKJB–NT). The reason for the existence of the United Nations is to establish peace. But the world's people cannot seem to foster peace among themselves or keep it for long. As I write these words, war rages along the Iraqi-Iranian border. The world has grown accustomed to conflict; but so long as the United States is not engaged in war, Americans lapse into a false security, thinking that the peace we enjoy within our own borders will not be affected by other conflicts.

In His Olivet discourse, Jesus warned that our world will experience a terrible time of affliction or pressure: "For in those days there will be tribulation, such as has not been from the beginning of creation, which God created to this time, nor ever shall be" (Mark 13:19 NKJB–NT). Mankind is experiencing this tribulation already in every realm these days—politically, economically, physically, mentally—and it will get worse. As the pressures mount, so will the longing for peace grow to such proportions that the peoples of the world will accept anything or anyone, just so they can be at peace. Such an attitude will be the perfect preparation for the "man of lawlessness," as Paul terms the Antichrist. "Let no one deceive you by any means;" Paul warned, "for that Day will not come unless the falling away comes first, and the man of sin is revealed, the son of perdition" (2 Thess. 2:3 NKJB–NT).

Cataclysmic Signs

According to the dictionary a cataclysm is "any violent change or upheaval, as a war or earthquake." It means literally a "flood." The world has already known one flood and we know that God promised never to destroy the earth again in that way. But Jesus did clearly predict multiple signs that would take place in the world, signaling the last days. He said, "For nation will rise against nation, and kingdom against kingdom. And there will be earthquakes in various places, and there will be famines and troubles. These are the beginnings of sorrows" (Mark 13:8 NKJB–NT). True, these have always been a part of our world's history. But no one can deny that war and earthquakes, floods and famine are a widespread and striking feature of the twentieth century. Together with what is happening in the Middle East, especially the rebirth of Israel, these take on unusual significance.

Jesus said further: "But in those days, after that tribulation, the sun will be darkened, and the moon will not give its light; the stars of heaven will fall, and the powers in heaven will be shaken'' (Mark 13:24,25 NKJB–NT). There are to be ''signs'' in the sun and moon and stars, according to Luke 21:25. Could this be a reference to man's exploration of the moon?

These cataclysmic signs are only a prelude to the utter destruction of the world as we know it. Peter prophesied: ''Looking for and hastening the coming of the day of God, on account of which the heavens will be destroyed by burning, and the elements will melt with intense heat!'' (2 Pet. 3:12).

Armageddon

In our day the ominous word *Armageddon* has become quite common. It rings with familiarity in the ears of almost everyone, though of course many people today do not have a clear idea of what it means. For centuries even theologians considered Armageddon a myth. Now we are on its threshold.

Volumes have been written to explain the war that is to take place in the future on the plain of Megiddo, between present-day Nazareth and the Mediterranean Sea. Scripture speaks of it in Revelation 16:16—''And they gathered them together to the place which in Hebrew is called Har-Magedon.'' History tells of battles and wars being fought on these plains, an area so vast that huge armies can be arrayed there against one another. Armageddon signifies a global confrontation, truly a world war. Related Scripture tells us that ''the number of the armies of the horsemen was two hundred thousand thousand [two hundred million]'' (Rev. 9:16). Today China is the only nation capable of mobilizing that many men. Many students of prophecy view the events in the Middle East now taking place as a prelude to a decisive struggle that would involve the Soviet Union in massive conflict against a revived, united Western Europe and China. Because of the accord now growing between the United States and China, some suggest the confrontation with the Soviets will erupt within this decade. Such a war would no doubt be a nuclear holocaust, a disaster which prophetic Scriptures seem to foretell!

Now this will be the plague with which the LORD will strike all the peoples who have gone to war against Jerusalem; their flesh will rot while they stand on their feet, and their eyes will rot in their sockets, and their tongue will rot in their mouth (Zech. 14:12).

Could there be a more graphic description of the horrors of nuclear war?

The Future Salvation of Israel

In the book of Zechariah we are informed five hundred years before Jesus' birth of the repentance of Israel:

And I will pour out on the house of David and on the inhabitants of Jerusalem, the Spirit of grace and of supplication, so that they will look on Me whom they have pierced; and they will mourn for Him, as one mourns for an only son, and they will weep bitterly over Him, like the bitter weeping over a first-born (12:10).

This prophecy could not have been fulfilled until after the coming of Christ. It appears to point to the same kind of widespread and far-reaching spiritual awakening spoken of in similar passages in Hosea, Amos, Micah, and elsewhere. Today Israel is wary but proud. She is riding high. Yet Zechariah 13:8,9 predicts:

"And it will come about in all the land,"
Declares the LORD,
"That two parts in it will be cut off and perish;
But the third will be left in it.
And I will bring the third part through the fire,
Refine them as silver is refined,
And test them as gold is tested.
They will call on My Name,

And I will answer them;
I will say, 'They are My people,'
And they will say, 'The LORD is my God.' ''

Ezekiel asserts that Israel will be changed by God's intervention.

"For I will take you from the nations, gather you from all the lands, and bring you into your own land. Then I will sprinkle clean water on you, and you will be clean; I will cleanse you from all your filthiness and from all your idols. Moreover, I will give you a new heart and put a new spirit within you; and I will remove the heart of stone from your flesh and give you a heart of flesh'' (36:24–26).

As a result of their discovery of Jesus as the true and only Messiah who will rescue them and save them, Israel (or more properly, the Jews) will become the new world missionaries. They are the 144,000 spoken of in Revelation 7:4 who will go throughout the world to testify, giving humanity a last chance to turn to God before the coming of judgment.

The Gospel Sign

All of these signs we have introduced in this chapter are on the verge of complete fulfillment. Israel's possession of Jerusalem could permit the Jews to rebuild the temple. The Golden Gate stands ready for its Messiah, and the Mount of Olives awaits its Master. Meanwhile, the world is growing desperate for peace as the earth rocks and reels under the strain of catastrophe and war. The way is being paved for Armageddon. Jewish evangelists note a marked willingness of the Jewish people to listen to the gospel. Actually one further sign awaits fulfillment.

This gospel of the kingdom shall be preached in all the world for a witness unto all nations; and then shall the end come (Matt. 24:14 KJV).

Even this sign of the universal proclamation of the gospel has unique relevance for our generation. At no time have so many Christians engaged themselves in the task of making Christ known throughout the world.

For what reason are there 60,000 missionaries around the world today? Why have there been in our time such challenging international conferences on evangelism as those held in Berlin, Lausanne, and most recently, in Thailand? Why has a vigorous organization such as Campus Crusade for Christ been raised up with a goal to preach Christ to the whole world by 1988? Why has the Southern Baptist Convention adopted a worldwide Bold Mission Thrust of world evangelization before the year 2000? Why are Trans World Radio from Monte Carlo and other missionary radio stations beaming the gospel in more than eighty languages with powerful transmitters that reach China, India, the U.S.S.R., and the Muslim world? Why has the church in our time been able to broadcast its message via satellite into television receivers around the world?

Glory to God, the answer can only be that God wants to tell the world that *Jesus is coming!*

But He will not return until every nation has had a chance to hear the good news. When we think of nations we think in terms of countries. We imagine their total, if we could enumerate them all, would approximate that of the membership of the United Nations. If this were so, we might feel comfortable about this final sign which Jesus said must be fulfilled, for there is in almost every country a church that is witnessing to the salvation that is in Jesus Christ. But we need only to look at the meaning of the New Testament Greek word for "nation" to understand what Jesus was really saying. The word "nation" is similar to our word "ethnic" and indicates people groups by culture, nationality, or tribe. Examining the nouns in Revelation 5:9 will help us see the meaning: ". . . for Thou wast slain, and didst purchase for God with Thy blood men from every tribe and tongue and people and nation.'' It is God's intention to offer salvation to every person.

One of the chief indicators that God is doing this today is the remarkable phenomenon of Bible translation work. In 1800 the Word of God existed in print in but 71 of the world's languages; by 1930 that figure had grown to 900. Now, some portion of the Word of God is available in published form in more than 1,685 languages! And Bible societies and groups like Wycliffe Bible Translators are at work in another thousand or so tongues. All of this means that the pace of world evangelization is quickening.

Still, a large number of the world's four billion people have never heard the name of Christ. We believers ought to weep over that fact. God taught me a lesson about this years ago when our daughter Deborah was born. We were living in Jordan and I was giving candy to friends in celebration of her birth when a missionary nurse on staff at Ajloun Baptist Hospital came to tell me that our daughter was dead. I cried to God, "Why? Why?" When my father was killed in Jordan in 1948 I had not cried, but I wept bitterly at the death of Deborah. Then God spoke to me through sorrow, heartache, and the book of Jonah.

"Why don't you shed tears, Anis, for those dead in sin all around you?" He asked me. I had no answer. There are people all around us in spiritual darkness and we are supposed to be the light of the world and the salt of the earth. Do we care? Are we trying to bring them to salvation? If we are, we are hastening the day when this sign is fulfilled and the Lord returns.

5

The Arabs in Prophecy

And as for Ishmael, I have heard you; behold, I will bless him, and will make him fruitful, and will multiply him exceedingly. He shall become the father of twelve princes, and I will make him a great nation.

(Gen. 17:20)

Most everyone, when asked the origin of the Arab peoples, replies that they sprang from Ishmael. That answer is only partially correct. Ishmael, the son of Abram, was the one to whom God promised fruitfulness and "a great nation," but he was not the sole progenitor of the Arabs.

In his later years Abraham, as he came to be known, took another wife when Sarah died. This woman, Keturah, gave Abraham six more sons and her offspring are recognized as among the earliest Arabs. Moses' wife, Zipporah, was a descendant of Abraham and Keturah.

A third strain of Arabian peoples traces its origin to Esau, twin brother of Jacob, grandson of Abraham. A lesser known, but important fourth strain grew from the descendants of Joktan, also known as Yoqtan or Qahtan (see Gen. 10:25–

53

29). A very early descendant of Noah, he was a son of Eber and a great-great-grandson of Shem. (See chart.) History books document that the descendants of Joktan peopled the southern regions of the Arabian peninsula, formed cities, and grew wealthy. The Queen of Sheba was of this people. The Ishmaelite Arabs roamed the great deserts in the northern part of the peninsula, from the Mediterranean to the Persian Gulf, and were typically nomads or bedouins.

Interestingly, scholars believe that the ancient name *Hebrews* is derived from Eber, the father of Joktan. Abraham came to be known as a Hebrew: "Then a fugitive came and told Abram the Hebrew. Now he was living by the oaks of Mamre the Amorite, brother of Eschol and brother of Aner, and these were allies with Abram" (Gen. 14:13).

God's Extraordinary Promises to Ishmael

Ishmael is easily the best recognized and most visible "father" of the Arab peoples. This is true, no doubt, because of the careful account given of Ishmael's birth and the promises of God concerning him as recorded in Scripture. At the age of eighty Sarai (as she was known before Isaac's birth) had not been able to give her husband any children. The marriage contract of those days dictated that another woman in the household could sleep with the husband to give him offspring. Abram did accept Hagar, the Egyptian handmaid of Sarai, and Hagar conceived. However, friction arose in the household and ultimately Hagar became despondent enough to leave (see Gen. 16:6).

Fearful and alone, Hagar wandered in the desert until the angel of the Lord appeared to her and instructed her to return to her mistress. The Lord told Hagar: "I will greatly multiply your descendants so that they shall be too many to count" (Gen. 16:10). Furthermore He named the child: "Behold, you are with child,/And you shall bear a son;/ And you shall call

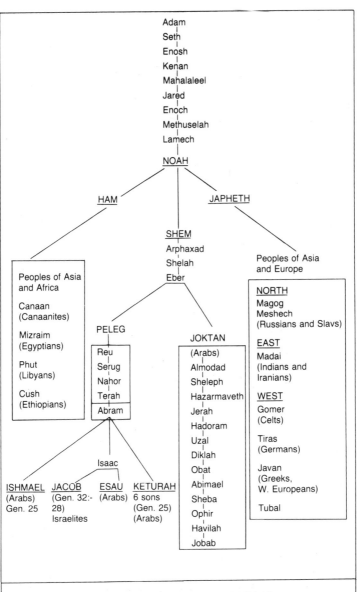

CHART OF THE NATIONS
Prepared by Anis Shorrosh

his name Ishmael,/Because the Lord has given heed to your affliction'' (v. 11). This incidentally was the first instance in recorded history of a name being given by divine direction before the child was born. The name Ishmael is derived from the same root word as Samuel and means that God hears or God answers. Although God would give Abraham and Sarai another son, Isaac, and make His eternal covenant with him, He would hear and answer Hagar.

But what was promised of Ishmael's character and his future as the angel continued to talk with Hagar must have disturbed the woman. ''He will be a wild man; his hand will be against every man, and every man's hand against him; and he shall dwell in the presence of all his brethren'' (Gen. 16:12 KJV).

Years passed and Ishmael was about thirteen when God told Abram that Isaac was to be born. ''. . . Oh that Ishmael might live before Thee!'' Abram argued (Gen. 17:18). He wanted God to fulfill His promises through Ishmael. So God, who had already made a strong promise to Hagar, makes an even stronger one to Abram concerning Ishmael:

And as for Ishmael, I have heard you; behold, I will bless him, and will make him fruitful, and will multiply him exceedingly. He shall become the father of twelve princes, and I will make him a great nation (Gen. 17:20).

God changed Abram's name to Abraham, ''father of a multitude.'' But to Abraham's astonishment, God said that the divine covenant would be through Isaac, not Ishmael.

Examining the prophetic blessings which God declared to Ishmael we cannot help but be impressed with their detailed fulfillment, even to the present day.

1. God declared that He would multiply Ishmael and make him fruitful. With the Arab peoples numbering 135 million today, God has obviously kept His word. Jews number only 16 million, leading some to wonder if God's blessings to

the Arabs far exceed those to the Jews, especially since both consider that the greater the number of descendants, the greater God's blessing.

2. God added in His promise that Ishmael would bring forth twelve princes or nations. Practically every Bible student is familiar with Jacob's twelve sons, but the twelve "princes" of Ishmael—his sons—are known only to a few. They are listed in Genesis 25:13–15: Nebaioth, Kedar, Adbeel, Mibsam, Mishma, Dumah, Massa, Hadad, Tema, Jetur, Naphish, and Kedemah. The Arab Information Office in New York City already lists an even greater number of Arab states: Algeria, Bahrain, Egypt, Iraq, Jordan, Kuwait, Lebanon, Libya, Mauritania, Morocco, Oman, Yemen (2), Qatar, Saudi Arabia, Somali, Sudan, Syria, Tunisia, and United Arab Emirates.[1]

3. God announced that ". . . I will make him a great nation." The Arab people have reason to feel that this particular promise of God has been fulfilled. With three million square miles of territory and two-thirds of the world's proven oil resources, they are rapidly becoming the wealthiest countries in the world.

When I was a lad in Palestine, my fellow students and I were taught the dream of creating a nation of Arabian states similar to the U.S.A. It has been a long-held dream. At the height of Arab influence in the world, in the seventh and eighth centuries, there was an international Arab empire, but since then the states have been held apart. Some progress toward an Arab nation has been made in this generation, but the cause of Arab unity is plagued by a fourth trait in their character also prophesied in Genesis.

4. Arab peoples are very independent. God said that Ishmael would be a "wild man" and "his hand will be against every man, and every man's hand against him. . . ." By and large the Arab people have managed to be free, maintaining their independence for most of the past 4000 years of recorded history. Yet the wars, uprisings, and rebellions that have plagued the Arabs are definitely a fulfillment of God's Word.

Egypt's Role in Prophecy

There are obvious connections between Egypt and the Arabs in the Bible. Hagar, an Egyptian girl, and Abraham became the best-known parents of the Arab peoples. And Ishmael, Hagar's son, took an Egyptian as his wife (see Gen. 21:21), thus cementing the relationship between that ancient nation and the Arab peoples.

Egypt figures largely in the history of the Old Testament, usually in one of two characterizations. She is either a place and a symbol of backsliding or of escape. Abram journeyed to Egypt because of famine in Palestine and there got himself in trouble (see Gen. 12:10), lying about his wife Sarai and failing to trust God. Later, Jacob's sons went to Egypt, again in a time of drought; and there found not only food for their family, but also their lost brother Joseph. Eventually, aged Jacob went to Egypt with all of his sons and the nation Israel was born there.

Centuries later, Jeroboam rebelled against King Solomon and fled to Egypt for safety (see 1 Kings 11:40). After Solomon's death, he returned and became king of the northern kingdom, Israel. When Jerusalem fell in 586 B.C. the prophet Jeremiah was forced to go into hiding in Egypt when the governor placed over the Jewish remnant rebelled against their Babylonian captors (see Jer. 43:6,7). Then, after the birth of the Christ child, Egypt once more served as a refuge when King Herod sought to kill all male children under two years old in Bethlehem (see Matt. 2:13).

Though throughout Israel's history Egypt was often her enemy, there were happier incidents. Joseph's two sons, Manasseh and Ephraim, were born to him of his Egyptian wife, Asenath, and they became the heads of two of the twelve tribes of Israel. What modern-day Israeli cannot see how closely the Jews' historic ties are with Egypt?

Until very recently, even the last three years, it has been difficult for students of the Bible to understand those Old Testament prophecies which speak of the future blessing of

Egypt. Not a few Christian scholars have had an argument with God over His promised goodness to these mortal enemies of the chosen people. Listen to the rather amazing things God said of Egypt through his prophet Isaiah:

In that day five cities in the land of Egypt will be speaking the language of Canaan and swearing allegiance to the LORD of hosts . . . . In that day there will be an altar to the LORD in the midst of the land of Egypt, and a pillar to the LORD near its border. And it will become a sign and a witness to the LORD of hosts in the land of Egypt; for they will cry to the LORD because of oppressors, and He will send them a Savior and a Champion, and He will deliver them. Thus the LORD will make Himself known to Egypt, and the Egyptians will know the Lord in that day. They will even worship with sacrifice and offering, and will make a vow to the LORD and perform it. And the LORD will strike Egypt, striking but healing; so they will return to the LORD, and He will respond to them and will heal them. In that day there will be a highway from Egypt to Assyria, and the Assyrians will come into Egypt and the Egyptians into Assyria, and the Egyptians will worship with the Assyrians. In that day Israel will be the third party with Egypt and Assyria, a blessing in the midst of the earth, whom the LORD of hosts has blessed, saying, "Blessed is Egypt My people, and Assyria the work of My hands, and Israel My inheritance" (Is. 19:18–25).

Wilbur Smith says of this chapter that it "contains the most important prophetic utterance concerning Egypt in all of the Old Testament. There is no basic theme of the predictions about Egypt that is not to be found here." [2]

Repeatedly, the prophet used the phrase "in that day," evidently pointing to the time of the millennium, when Christ will rule on earth. And for that time he predicts blessings of incalculable proportion. The Lord uses the loving expression "My people"—usually reserved only for Israel—in speaking of Egypt. He pledges His word that Israel, Egypt, and Assyria (modern Iraq) will be a threefold "blessing in the midst of the earth." Is the signing of the peace treaty between Egypt and Israel a step toward the fulfillment of that prophecy?

I was in Texas seeking revival with the First Baptist Church of Daingerfield when the Camp David agreement was signed in September 1978. A friend called me, urging me to fly immediately to Egypt and begin a revival effort because he believed the words spoken in verse 21 were being fulfilled.

Thus the LORD will make Himself known to Egypt, and the Egyptians will know the LORD in that day. They will even worship with sacrifice and offering, and will make a vow to the LORD and perform it.

On October 25, 1980, "President Anwar Sadat inaugurated a $140 million, 3.2-mile automobile tunnel under the Suez Canal," reported the New York *Daily News*. He "hailed it as a strategic achievement providing the first land link in more than 100 years between the east and west of the Muslim world saying 'Today I rejoice in a maximum sense of achievement because this tunnel ends the isolation of Sinai from Egypt forever.' "[3] This tunnel could be a partial fulfillment of the promise in verse 23 of "a highway from Egypt to Assyria."

How strange that the Arabs control three million square miles of land but cannot allow Israel, their kinfolk, to have ten thousand square miles. The hallowed parcel of land, Palestine, has actually been in the hands of Arab peoples longer than it has been controlled by the descendants of Jacob. Yet God promised it to the Israelites.

And the LORD said to Abram, after Lot had separated from him, "Now lift up your eyes and look from the place where you are, northward and southward and eastward and westward; for all the land which you see, I will give it to you and to your descendants forever. And I will make your descendants as the dust of the earth; so that if anyone can number the dust of the earth, then your descendants can also be numbered" (Gen. 13:14–16).

This covenant He confirmed to Isaac in Genesis 26:3,4.

"Sojourn in this land and I will be with you and bless you, for to you and to your descendants I will give all these lands, and I will establish the oath which I swore to your father Abraham. And I will multiply your descendants as the stars of heaven, and will give your descendants all these lands; and by your descendants all the nations of the earth shall be blessed."

In fact, according to Genesis 15:18 and Jeremiah 23:7,8, the promise will eventually cover 180,000 square miles from Egypt's river to the Euphrates. It is my opinion that this will be fulfilled soon, either within this decade or in the millennium.

The Arabs Yesterday

There are many reasons why the people of the Western nations are so ignorant of the Arabs. First, when the Arab world was at its zenith, Europe was under the burden of the Dark Ages. Westerners did not realize that while they lived in mud huts and had open drainage in their cities, people in Baghdad and Damascus were building palaces and drainage systems. The papacy, which was predominant in Europe, refused to acknowledge that "pagans" were capable of advances in any important field—literature, medicine, or philosophy. Those areas in which incredible advances were being made by Arab peoples, the sciences, were discounted by the hierarchy of Europe as less important or threatening to true wisdom.

Another reason for ignorance, a very natural one, may be added—the language barrier. As Latin was the language of the scholar in Europe during Arab ascendancy, from the seventh to twelfth century, the language of Africa and the Middle East was Arabic. Written Arabic dates to the time of the rise of Islam. As that religion spread, Arabic became the common medium of expression from Persia to the Pyrenees. One writer says that "the warriors who came out of the Arabian peninsula brought with them a remarkably flexible language, capable of developing new words to meet new situations." [4] Actually many English words, such as *alphabet* and *algebra,* originated in Arabic. It is a rich language, containing for instance 350 different words for camel and 150 words for fire. Muslims believe that Allah chose Arabic as the language of the Holy Koran because of its richness.

Certainly the Arabs have always preached that there is only one God. However far the Arabs have wandered from the truth—most Arabs are Muslims—they have faithfully introduced monotheism wherever they have gone.

Even in the fields in which Europeans presumed they were dominant, medicine, literature and philosophy, the Arab contribution has actually been vital to Western development. In medicine, for example, Arab doctors and surgeons were unmatched for skill and knowledge during the Middle Ages. Avicenna, also known as Ibn Sina, is still cited in medical textbooks and encyclopedias. He was famous for his work as an astronomer, poet, and philosopher, but especially as a physician. His *Canun* of medicine was used for six hundred years as a textbook. A prolific author who lived A.D. 980–1037, Avicenna authored sixty-eight books on theology and philosophy, eleven on astronomy, sixteen on medicine, and four on poetry.

Jabir ibn Hayyan, the accomplished chemist of the eighth century, may well have been the discoverer of nitric and sulphuric acids. From Arabs, Europeans learned how to extract sugar from sugar cane and how to make syrup. Al-Haythum of Cairo founded the science of optics and left to posterity some of the earliest careful descriptions of the eye's structure, optical illusions, mirages, and binocular vision.

In history and literature Arabs also hold a great place of honor among men. It was of Ibn Khaldun that Arnold Toynbee said: "His philosophy of history is the greatest work of its kind that has ever yet been created by any mind any time." Ibn Khaldun proved that events were shaped by religious beliefs, customs, climates, and racial backgrounds. He lived in the fourteenth century.

The Rubaiyat of Omar Khayyam is still studied in university literature classes some nine centuries after Khayyam lived. Edward Fitzgerald, the gifted translator who gave this epic poem to the Western world, fostered the idea that Khayyam was chiefly a poet. In his day he was actually better known as a mathematician.

Who can forget *The Arabian Nights,* which undoubtedly influenced Jonathan Swift's *Gulliver's Travels?* It is attested by many that a twelfth-century Arab, Yaqzan, wrote the first novel, *Alive, Son of Awake.* Daniel Defoe is thought to have read this novel when he visited Morocco and gained from it the inspiration for his *Robinson Crusoe.*

Ancient Arabs made significant advances in mathematics and astronomy. Of course, their crowning contribution to modern man is the simple system of Arabic numerals and the zero. Rom Landau, in his book *The Arab Heritage of Western Civilization,* says, "Had the Arabs given us nothing but the decimal system, their contribution to progress would have been considerable. In actual fact they gave us infinitely more." He adds: "The men who advanced Western mathematical and astronomical knowledge sufficiently to enable us today to send rockets to the moon were Keppler, Copernicus, Galileo, and Newton. Yet none of these could have arrived at his scientific conclusions had it not been for the spadework done several hundred years earlier by the Arab mathematicians and astronomers."[5] James and Marti Hefley (who authored my biography, *The Liberated Palestinian*) make similar claims for the Arabs in their book *Arabs, Christians and Jews.*

Six centuries before Galileo, the Italian astronomer Al-Biruni declared that the earth rotated on its axis. Yunus used the pendulum at Cairo centuries before Galileo was born. In the eleventh century al-Zarkali prepared planetary tables, calling them *Tables of Toledo,* for it was in that city of Spain that he lived and worked. Astronomers for centuries after him used these tables in determining the positions of the planets.

The Arab, Idris, prepared *Roger's Book* for King Roger II

of Normandy. Complete with seventy maps, it was the first world atlas. Yagut of Baghdad compiled the forerunner of our modern encyclopedia, arranging geographical, biographical, and scientific information in alphabetical order.

In the ninth century, al-Khwarizmi utilized concepts of algebra developed earlier by Greek, Hindu, and Arab scholars. Along with other Arab scholars he used the positive and negative signs and developed fractions much as we use them now. Algebra was developed as a science by the Arabs, though it was not known and used in Europe until the sixteenth century.

Probably the greatest center of learning in the entire world from the ninth to the eleventh centuries was Baghdad. Caliph Mamoun established there the House of Wisdom, a place where Arab scholars translated and commented on the works of Socrates, Aristotle, Plato, Pythagoras, Euclid, and Hippocrates. Without these Arabic translations, the works of the great Greek philosophers might have been lost to the world.

As did al-Khwarizmi, other Arabs mined the Greek philosophers who went before them. When Nestorian monks fled Catholic persecution to Persia, Arab scholars helped the monks translate their writings and make them available to the Arab world.

In the twelfth century, when the armies of Christian Europe conquered the Muslim Moors in Spain, those Europeans who could read Arabic were astounded by what they found. In the abandoned cities and libraries were treasures of Arabic poetry, literature, and scientific writings. Catholic Archbishop Raymond, like Caliph Mamoun of Baghdad, established an academy for translation in Toledo. European scholars translated the Arabic works first into Latin and then into the language of Europe's ethnic groups. This is thought to have stimulated the desire for translations of the Bible into the vernacular of the people which, of course, led to the Reformation, the Renaissance, and the discovery of the New World. Incidentally, the man who interpreted for Christopher Columbus on the voyage of the *Santa Maria* to America was a Spanish Arab.

The Arabs Today

Just as "sons of Ishmael" have made their mark on the world in the past, they are doing so today. If people were asked who among Arab peoples today has had the greatest impact on our world, the majority would say Anwar el-Sadat, the late president of Egypt. This dynamic and compassionate man captured the attention of the world with his bold trip to Jerusalem, changing, at least for a time, how Americans viewed the Arab world. After his historic trip in 1977 a poll showed that 86 percent of Americans believed his peace initiative had increased the prospects for peace; 40 percent of those surveyed said that their impressions of Egypt had improved.

There are other leading Arab figures. Jordan's King Hussein has been the head of his government longer than any Arab head of state. Though he is not admired in much of the world, Yasser Arafat of the P.L.O. (Palestinian Liberation Organization) is regarded as a hero of the downtrodden Palestinian Arabs.

Arabs are making a mark as leaders in other fields also. In America, some two million Arabs make their home, the majority of them having obtained American citizenship. In show business, the Arab-American Danny Thomas is well known. In politics, the Honorable James Abouresk serves as a senator from the state of South Dakota. Dr. Sami Hamarni of Jordan is in a responsible position with the Smithsonian Institute in Washington, D.C. Many Arab doctors follow in the tradition of Avicenna, among whom is Dr. Kamal Mansour of Egypt, now on the staff of Emory University Medical School in Atlanta. Among Christian Arabs of renown is Dr. John Haggai, a Baptist evangelist and educator, whose parents emigrated from Syria around the turn of the century.

What can unite these gifted peoples? Can their animosity

for Israel? When nations of the West continued to lend their support to the state of Israel, angry Arab nations initiated the oil embargo of 1973. When the flow of the precious liquid resumed, the price kept escalating until in 1979 it was twelve times what it was in 1970. That in turn unleashed the most terrible inflation of modern time. Saudi Arabia alone is said to receive $6.8 million more *each hour* than it can spend. At that rate they could purchase all of the Rockefeller holdings in six days and all the stock on the world's stock exchanges in fifteen years. The Saudis now own $30 billion in American bonds. But even with their wealth and their common hatred for the Zionist state, they are not a united people.

Their geography is a unifying factor, gathered as they are along the Mediterranean and at the junction of Africa and Asia. Their culture and their religion also are unifying factors, although within Islam there are strong divisive factions. The strongest common denominator among Arabs is the language. Though the dialects are numerous, classical or literary Arabic is one and the same whether one lives in Amman, Beirut, Cairo, or Jerusalem.

The great need among my native people is not wealth or culture or language or even religion. As an Arab I found peace within and a love for my fellow man and even for the Jew when I truly surrendered my life to Jesus Christ as Savior and Lord. Love of the Lord Jesus is the answer for my Arab people. From Jesus I learned:

You have heard that it was said, "You shall love your neighbor, and hate your enemy." But I say to you, love your enemies, and pray for those who persecute you in order that you may be sons of your Father who is in heaven . . . (Matt. 5:43–45).

6

War Over Jordan

What is this you are doing? Why are you living in the cities of the Jews? Aren't the Jews enough to fill them up? Didn't they inherit them from me? Why then have you, who worship Milcom, taken over Gad and all its cities? I will punish you for this, the Lord declares, by destroying your city of Rabbah. It shall become a desolate heap, and the neighboring towns shall be burned. Then Israel shall come and take back her land from you again. She shall dispossess those who dispossessed her, says the Lord.

Cry out, O Heshbon, for Ai is destroyed! Weep, daughter of Rabbah! Put on garments of mourning; weep and wail, hiding in the hedges, for your god Milcom shall be exiled along with his princes and priests. You are proud of your fertile valleys, but they will soon be ruined. O wicked daughter, you trusted in your wealth and thought no one could ever harm you. But see, I will bring terror upon you, says the Lord God of Hosts. For all your neighbors shall drive you from your land and none shall help your exiles as they flee. But afterward I will restore the fortunes of the Ammonites, says the Lord.

(Jer. 49:1–6 TLB)

Jordan is the focus of this passage, given here in *The Living Bible*. Jordan is the land of the ancient Ammonites. One can see a linguistic link between the name of these Arab peoples and the name of the capital and chief city of Jordan—Amman.

Speaking through his prophet Jeremiah, the Lord declares a coming judgment on the Ammonites and tells of a day when Israel will "dispossess those who dispossessed her." In our study of prophecy and the Middle East, we now turn to the question of Jordan, the coming war, and Jordan's subsequent revival. It is a piece of the Middle East puzzle.

Ammonites, Edomites, and Moabites were in the land now known as Syria and Jordan before the people of Israel were delivered from Egypt. They opposed the Israelite conquest of the Promised Land and in the ensuing centuries were among Israel's mortal enemies. Later, as Israel sinned against God and forsook His commands, the Lord used these Arab peoples to bring judgment on His people. It was the kingdom of Assyria that subdued Israel in the eighth century.

From the fourth century until 63 B.C., Syria and most of Palestine were ruled by the Greeks. After Alexander the Great's death, the Seleucids took possession of the northern part of Palestine and founded ten cities ("The Decapolis"), one of which was Philadelphia—modern-day Amman. Rome gained the upper hand in 63 B.C. and for the next six centuries ancient Syria and its Arab neighbors were a province of the Roman Empire. But the Arab peoples remained in the land. In the seventh century, as Rome's fortunes waned, Muslim Arabs from the Arabian peninsula brought to Palestine the message of Muhammad. From that time this part of the Middle East has been predominantly Muslim in religion. The Ottoman Turks ruled the region from the ninth century until 1918, with the exception of a brief interval when Christian armies during the tragic Crusades fought and overwhelmed the Arabs.

With the defeat of the Turks in World War I, the Allies partitioned the Ottoman Empire. France occupied Syria and Lebanon and the British took Palestine, Iraq, and Transjordan. The latter was so named because it consisted of the region on the east side of the Jordan River. As did the other Allies,

The incredibly beautiful Dome of the Rock in the midst of the ancient Temple area.
The tiny gray dome on the right is possibly the ancient site of the Holy of Holies.

Will this sacred mosque have to go before the rebuilt temple takes shape? Read Rev. 11:1-2.

Mt. Olives with Garden of Gethsemane as seen from the Eastern Gate--Joel 3:2. Zechariah 14:4 says the Mt. will split.

The Western Wall of Herod's Temple, formerly called "The Wailing Wall." The author believes the new temple will be rebuilt in this area very soon.

The other side of the important Golden Gate in the Eastern Wall of Jerusalem. It will open when Jesus returns.

The lovely Golden Gate, also called The Eastern Gate. The order to reopen it in 1966, by Jordan, caused the author to reexamine his position on prophecy. Read Ezekiel 44:1-2.

View of the Plains of Megiddo at sunset. I was on top of Mt. Tabor when I took the picture. Rev. 16:16.

Relics of the 1967 war near Megiddo.

On the spot check by Israeli armed forces on a Jericho road.

The world famous Jerusalem Bazaars are a shopper's paradise.

Shrine of the Book Museum is where the Dead Sea Scrolls and other artifacts are preserved in West Jerusalem.

Nazareth, hometown of Jesus, with Church of Annunciation rising majestically from the center of town. The author of this book was born and raised in Nazareth.

The calm, cool and charming Jordan River is a paradox. It has become a bloody barrier between the warring Sons of Abraham. It separates Jordan from Israel.

Britain maintained control over its region, assigning the powers of government to Arab rulers or *emirs*. Eventual independence was promised to these emirs and their kingdoms.

The peninsula of Arabia was given to Abdulaziz Al Saud, the founder of modern Saudi Arabia. Several decades passed before the world recognized that Arabia contained some of the world's richest oilfields. When the Allies gave the land to King Aziz they believed it to be worthless desert sand.

Egypt was the first of the Middle East territories to gain its independence, achieving it in 1922 though Britain reserved the right to keep troops there to protect the Suez Canal. What was to become modern Iraq was placed under the rule of King Faisal Al Hussein. Britain also promised Syria, Palestine, Jordan, and Lebanon to King Faisal; but secretly the heads of government in Great Britain, France, and the Soviet Union had entered into the Sykes-Picot Agreement which took precedence over the negotiations signed with the Arab chieftain. Arab confidence in British intentions suffered a severe blow. Eventually, in 1932, Iraq received its independence. Lebanon and Syria became independent of France in 1943 and 1946, respectively. British troops withdrew in 1956 when President Nasser of Egypt nationalized the Suez Canal.

Jordan's Rebirth

Abdullah Al Hussein, brother of Faisal, took the throne as emir of the newly formed Transjordan territory in 1921. Ninety percent of the land was desert. The Sykes-Picot Agreement, the British mandate which Abdullah administered, included half of Palestine as a reward to Abdullah. When Transjordan gained its full independence in 1946, Abdullah assumed the title of king and the name of the nation officially changed to the Hashemite Kingdom of Jordan. Soon the ancient rivalry between Arab and Jew was to test the strength of the new Arab republics and boundary changes were to follow.

The United Nations had decreed in 1947 that Palestine was to be partitioned, half for the Arabs and half for the Jews. In 1948 when the British mandate in Palestine ended, Israel declared itself an independent nation, inciting the war between Israel and all of her Arab neighbors. Abdullah's military forces had been trained by the brilliant British general, John B. Glubb, known popularly as "Glubb Pasha." Contrary to the new king's hopes, these forces were not able to defeat the valiant Israeli army. Fighting continued until a truce was secured by the United Nations in January 1949. Even though Israel had gained much territory in what is now known as the "West Bank," Jordan retained possession of Jerusalem and such ancient cities of Palestine as Samaria, Jericho, Bethlehem, and Ramallah.

King Abdullah's reign was to be short-lived. In 1951 while on his way to worship in the Muslim mosque of Al-Aqsa in Jerusalem, an assassin killed him. Rumors had spread that the king was dealing directly with the hated nation of Israel and many Palestinians felt avenged at his death. Abdullah's son, Prince Talal, succeeded to the throne but was removed from office because of mental illness. His seventeen-year-old son, Hussein, became the new king. Having survived many attempts on his life in the nearly three decades of his reign, King Hussein is recognized as one of the ablest rulers in the troubled Middle East. He is not physically large; his height is only five feet four inches. But his escapes from some twenty assassination attempts are legendary and really miraculous. Many believe that God is protecting him to prevent the chaos his death would cause in Jordan.

Jeremiah's Prophecy Fulfilled

One method of study employed by the Hebrews is to examine the last verse in a passage first and then to work one's way backward to the beginning of the passage. Following that method, consider verses 5 and 6 in the prophecy quoted at the beginning of this chapter.

For all your neighbors shall drive you from your land and none shall help your exiles as they flee. But afterward I will restore the fortunes of the Ammonites, says the Lord.

Having briefly traced the history of the nation of Jordan, we must not miss the significance of what has happened. Nations come and go and more have gained their autonomy in our generation than at any other time in the history of man. But this rebirth of Jordan—ancient Ammon—is a fulfillment of prophecy just as surely as is the rebirth of Israel! The Ammonites were a dead nation; yet God's Word declared that both Jordan and Israel will rise—and they have risen!

The United States has supported Jordan more substantially than did the British. Few Americans are familiar with the Jordan River Valley Authority, but it was one of the most auspicious and far-reaching projects attempted with U.S. aid in the Middle East. The plan called for $32 million worth of construction to erect dams on the Yarmuk River, which empties into the beautiful Jordan River a few miles southeast of the Sea of Galilee. These dams brought irrigation to thousands of acres of arid lands and enabled Jordanian agriculturists to produce two and three crops each year. The Jordan Valley is a natural hothouse, being more than seven hundred feet below sea level. Produce from there is shipped by truck all over the Middle East and by air to Kuwait, Saudi Arabia, and even to England.

The Scriptures further say:

"Therefore behold, the days are coming," declares the LORD,
"That I shall cause a trumpet blast of war to be heard
Against Rabbah of the sons of Ammon;
And it will become a desolate heap,
And her towns will be set on fire.

Then Israel will take possession of his possessors,"
Says the LORD
(v. 2).

This is exactly what happened in the Six Day War in 1967. Israel took over the entire West Bank which Jordan had controlled since the two nations were born. Despite the Sykes-Picot Agreement, there is a more ancient and binding document that is to be followed—the Holy Scriptures.

The city of Rabbah (v. 2) is none other than modern-day Amman. It takes its name from the Ammonites, having been called Rabbath-Ammon in Old Testament times. Today it is a large metropolis of 750,000 people teeming with thousands of poor Palestinian refugees. It is also a haven for many affluent citizens of Beirut who have had to flee for their lives because of the terrible civil war in Lebanon. In 1948 Amman was a desert town with one paved street, though its long past was evident in the ruins. One can still see the fourth-century ruins of an ancient Roman amphitheater in the heart of the city. The Seleucids established this city sometime after 300 B.C. (and called it Philadelphia), but it is thought that an even earlier city on that site was desolated by warring forces prior to that. Jeremiah's prophecy, dated to the sixth century B.C., could refer to the desolation that took place after Israel's fall—or does it point to a yet future judgment to descend on Amman?

In verse 1 the Lord speaks, "What is this you are doing? Why are you living in the cities of the Jews?" Relating this prophecy to modern times, it is a fact that Jordanians controlled more than a third of ancient Palestine. "Aren't the Jews enough to fill them up?" The truth is that in 1948, when Israel declared itself an independent nation, there were not enough Jews to fill up the land of Palestine. Hardly 650,000 Jews had immigrated to Palestine. Jordan held control of a portion of Palestine almost twenty years, only relinquishing the territory when forced to do so in the Six Day War. By then Israel's Jewish population had increased to approximately three million. There were clearly enough Jews to "fill up" the land.

The Future of Jordan

"Wail, O Heshbon, for Ai has been destroyed!
Cry out, O daughters of Rabbah,
Gird yourselves with sackcloth and lament,
And rush back and forth inside the walls;
For Malcam will go into exile
Together with his priests and his princes"
(v. 3).

This Scripture, I believe, utilizes symbolic terms. The name Ai stands for ancient Palestine. The city is best known as the site of Israel's first defeat when entering the Promised Land and battling with its pagan inhabitants. In that story (see Joshua 7) the city of Ai is treated as an easy object for Israel's victorious armies. It is certainly presented as less powerful than the city of Jericho. But ancient ruins that have been unearthed at Ai by archaeologists reveal that Ai was once quite a stronghold. Excavations have uncovered double walls thick enough for two chariots to ride upon side by side. Architectural designs show that long before Jerusalem became prominent, the rulers of Egypt had built Ai on the grand scale of the pharaohs and had made it the capital of their Palestinian province. Archaeological remains date to approximately 2200 B.C.

If Ai symbolizes ancient Palestine, and we know that Palestine was taken by Israel in the Six Day War, what does Heshbon signify? Our text says, "Wail, O Heshbon, for Ai . . . !" In Hebrew grammar a common technique is to repeat a thought, slightly rephrased, to declare the author's meaning. The next phrase in our text is "Cry out, O daughters of Rabbah . . . ." Since we know that Rabbah symbolizes Amman, the center of modern Jordan, perhaps this Scripture foretells a coming war against Jordan in which Israel will gain control over all or most of Jordan.

When would such a war take place? No one knows. Vyndal Jones, who assisted me very ably in helping me understand this prophecy, thinks it will happen soon. It could be that the king of Jordan, in a major revolution, will be forced to leave the country as did the Shah of Iran. He would not be killed; it seems more likely that he will abandon the throne and flee with his top aides. The Palestinian refugees, who have been a people without a country for so long, tried unsuccessfully in 1971 to topple the government in Jordan. Perhaps they will try again and succeed. Since half of the population of Jordan is comprised of Palestinians, that does not seem unreasonable.

Such a conflict could provoke Israel to retaliate and bring about a bloody war that would leave both sides devastated. The prospects of such a showdown are becoming more pronounced with the growing strength of the Palestinian Liberation Organization (P.L.O.). Hasn't their leader, Yasser Arafat, declared: "Today Iran, tomorrow Palestine!" With sophisticated military equipment now available to the P.L.O. and with tensions mounting in the already unstable Middle East, an ugly conflict could break out very soon.

But, in summary, let us not forget the truly amazing revival of Jordan. In our lifetime, the modern descendants of the Ammonites have been restored to a kingdom and the nation Jordan has been born. It is no less a miracle than the restoration of Israel.

7

Mystery of the Withered Fig Tree Solved

And Jesus came out from the temple and was going away when His disciples came up to point out the temple buildings to Him. And He answered and said to them, "Do you not see all these things? Truly I say to you, not one stone here shall be left upon another, which will not be torn down." And as He was sitting on the Mount of Olives, the disciples came to Him privately, saying, "Tell us, when will these things be, and what will be the sign of Your coming, and of the end of the age?" . . . "Now learn the parable from the fig tree: when its branch has already become tender, and puts forth its leaves, you know that summer is near; even so you too, when you see all these things, recognize that He is near, right at the door.

(Matt. 24:1–3,32,33)

During the three years I was pastor of a young international church in Jerusalem, more than once I went up on the Mount of Olives to pray. One night in 1966 I was praying on its crest near a large hotel. The hotel watchman turned his flashlight toward me and shouted, "What are you doing down there?" As he came closer he recognized me.

"I know who you are," he blurted out. "You picked me up the other day on the highway, when my car had run out of fuel, bought gas for the car, and told me about Jesus! But what are you doing here?"

"Look at our city," I told him, pointing to the Temple Mount and to the metropolis beyond. "I'm praying for our city."

The night watchman seemed a bit puzzled. "You know," he said, "you are a strange man. I've never seen anyone do that before."

Of course what I did isn't strange at all. I'm sure that some Christian residents of the city pray for its people. But I think that the reason for the lack of miracles and the lack of the presence of God in Jerusalem and other cities is that not many are shedding tears in intercessory prayer for people who are frustrated, fearful, and famished.

I often wondered if I were in the same spot on the Mount where our Lord prayed and spoke to His disciples and told them of the signs to come. It was but a few days before His crucifixion. On that occasion His disciples asked Him three questions:

1. When will Jerusalem be destroyed?
2. What will be the sign of Jesus' second coming?
3. When will the world—or the age—come to an end?

For years I grouped the three questions into one, and I was confused as I read further in the chapter, trying to make sense out of it. Much of my confusion evaporated when I realized that there are really three questions here and that Jesus addresses Himself to each concern.

When Will Jerusalem Be Destroyed?

From our vantage point, the question regarding the destruction of Jerusalem does not seem extraordinary. History tells us that the Roman armies under Titus sacked Jerusalem in 70 A.D. and burned it to the ground. But the destruction of their great city was the farthest thing from the minds of the Jews of Jesus' day. In the passage under consideration (see Matt. 24, Mark 13, Luke 21) it is evident that the disciples were justly proud of Jerusalem. One can almost see them scanning the impressive lines of the temple as they spoke of them to Jesus. Since a few years had passed since the magnificent temple, built under King Herod the Great, had been completed, additional construction was still going on along the entrance ways. It was an imposing sight. Imagine the surprise of the disciples when Jesus said, ''not one stone here shall be left upon another, which will not be torn down.''

In His explanation that followed, I believe Jesus gave the disciples the answer they sought, to the very year. Luke tells us that Jesus answered: ''. . . 'Jerusalem will be trampled underfoot by the Gentiles until the times of the Gentiles be fulfilled' '' (Luke 21:24). In Hebrew, the phrase ''trampled underfoot by the Gentiles'' is *Yerushalam Tel*, meaning ''Jerusalem will become a heap.'' Archaeologists use the term *tel* so commonly that most everyone knows its meaning immediately. *Tel*, a manmade mound, refers to the historic practice of conquering armies who would plunder and burn a city, leaving all the remains in a heap of rubble.

In time, weeds and scrub brush take over such a site, and with the passing of more time, all that survives is a mound. In the last two centuries hundreds of these *tels* have yielded to the picks and shovels of the archaeologists, opening up hidden treasures and revealing much about life in earlier times. Jesus prophesied that Jerusalem would be *Yerushalam Tel*.

The Hebrew alphabet numbers twenty-two characters and each has a numerical significance. The letter *aleph* is the figure

1, *beth* is 2, *gimel* is 3, and so on (see chart). When the value of the characters in a word or phrase is summed up, it often conveys a hidden meaning—a given date or the number in an army or an amount of gold.

When Jesus said Gentiles would make a heap of Jerusalem, His listeners could have determined the exact year this would happen if they had added up the equivalent value of the words, *Yerushalam Tel*. The sum of those letters is 3830 or, when translated into the chronology of the Gregorian calendar, A.D. 70! Thus Jesus provided His listeners with the precise year of Jerusalem's destruction and the Jewish dispersion. History and biblical prophecy complement each other because history is actually His story.

What Is the Sign of His Coming?

Whether they knew it or not, the disciples were right in asking Jesus for the singular, particular sign that would foreshadow His coming. Elsewhere He spoke of signs, and we have treated many of them in the earlier pages of this book. But I believe the Spirit led the disciples to ask for the *one* sign—above all other signs—that would point the way to His second coming. And Jesus gave them an answer in the form of a parable. Our generation in particular should be able to interpret that sign because of one world event that has taken place.

Now learn the parable from the fig tree: when its branch has already become tender, and puts forth its leaves, you know that summer is near; even so you too, when you see all these things, recognize that He is near, *right* at the door. Truly I say to you, this generation will not pass away until all these things take place (Matt. 24:32–34).

To understand what Jesus was talking about, it is necessary to know what He meant by the "fig tree." What is the fig

THE HEBREW ALPHABET

The Hebrew alphabet consists of 22 consonants. They are:

Form		Name	Transliteration	Numerical Value
	Finals			
א		'Áleph	'	1
ב	בּ	Bêth, Bhêth	b, bh	2
ג	גּ	Gímel, Ghímel	g, gh	3
ד	דּ	Dáleth, Dháleth	d, dh	4
ה		Hē	h	5
ו		Wāw	w	6
ז		Záyin	z	7
ח		Ḥêth	ḥ	8
ט		Ṭêth	ṭ	9
י		Yôdh	y	10
כּ כ ך		Kaph, Khaph	k, kh	20
ל		Lámedh	l	30
מ ם		Mêm	m	40
נ ן		Nûn	n	50
ס		Sámekh	s	60
ע		'Áyin	'	70
פּ פ ף		Pē, Phē	p, ph	80
צ ץ		Ṣádhê	ṣ	90
ק		Qôph	q	100
ר		Rêš	r	200
שׁ שׂ		Śîn, Šîn	ś, š	300
ת תּ		Tāw, Thāw	t, th	400

tree? It is generally accepted that Israel is symbolized because in numerous passages in the Old Testament God speaks of His chosen people as a fig tree (see Jer. 24:1–8; 29:17; Hos. 9:10).

But why would Jesus call their attention to the fig tree? To answer that we look at an earlier passage, Matthew 21:19, where Jesus spoke to a fig tree which was alongside the road as He and His disciples walked toward Jerusalem. The fig tree withered "at once." This incident took place in the tiny village of Bethpage which means "village of unripened figs." Fig trees were everywhere, but one was singled out to be the object lesson for the disciples.

From this reference to a fig tree, I believe Jesus intended to demonstrate to His disciples just how swiftly the destruction of the Jewish people would take place. Indeed, it was hardly thirty-seven years later when Jerusalem was destroyed.

The purpose of the fig tree is to bear fruit; yet that tree was barren. Indeed, the Jewish nation which should have been bringing forth fruit to the glory of God had rejected its Creator and was barren. Now for twenty centuries it has continued to reject the Messiah. And why? Was not the Messiah a Jew? Were not the first church members Jews? The popular song "Wasted Years" fits the Jews better than any other people, for they have wasted approximately two thousand years waiting for a Messiah who has already come!

So, Jesus judged the fig tree because He found no fruit on its branches. He had entered Jerusalem on the first day of the week, what we call Palm Sunday. On the following day He cursed the fig tree. And His Olivet discourse took place the next day. He was trying to tell the disciples that the nation Israel would be dead and remain dead until the living God moved in history and performed a miracle. The miracle would baffle all of the politicians and diplomats, historians and sociologists—Jews and Arabs. And in 1948 it happened. Israel arose from the "valley of dry bones" and became a nation. There is no way apart from the prophetic, eschatological view that the rebirth of Israel can be explained. The disciples wanted to know what was the most significant and specific sign that would trigger the countdown to the coming of Jesus and He told them: the reestablishment of Israel as a nation in the land of Palestine. We can see that it has happened right before our eyes!

Birth and Early Years

The birth of Israel was preceded by many events and historic steps. One of the most decisive came in 1917 when the British government announced its intention to create a homeland for the Jews. This has become known as the Balfour Declaration:

His Majesty's Government view with favor the establishment, in Palestine, of a national home for the Jewish people, and will use their best endeavour to facilitate the achievement of this object, it being clearly understood that nothing shall be done which may prejudice the civil and religious rights of existing non-Jewish communities in Palestine or the rights and political status enjoyed by Jews in any other country.[1]

The effect of this declaration was not felt immediately. Jews were not in a hurry to migrate to Palestine, except from the places where life was difficult for them. But during the 1930s and early '40s this trickle became a flood as millions could not bear to see their fellow Jews imprisoned and put to death. The horrors of the Nazi Holocaust prepared the hearts of the Jews; they began to return to their homeland by the shipload so that by 1948 there were 650,000 Jews in Palestine. In 1900 there had been only 52,000.

Now take note of another important fact. Jesus said, "Truly I say to you, this generation will not pass away until all these things take place." The word "generation" can be interpreted "this newborn one." In other words, Jesus was saying that "this newborn one" would survive to see all these other signs take place—wars, earthquakes, famine, pestilence, immorality, and the universal proclamation of the gospel.

In 1958 Israel minted a very interesting commemorative coin. The nation was ten years old and the coin was a part of the anniversary celebration. One side of the coin shows a Roman soldier holding a sword over a woman who is on her knees. This was to symbolize the destruction of Jerusalem by Titus. The year etched on the edge of the coin is 3830 in Hebrew letters, *GDDL,* which is the equivalent of A.D. 70. The reverse side shows an old man planting a fig tree and across from him is a woman lifting up a baby in her arms to God. No longer is she in servitude and humiliation. The baby is symbolic of the newborn nation of Israel.

According to Jewish custom, there are five stages of growth in the life of a Jew. First is birth and the early years. When a baby is born he is called "a child of blood" because he is born through blood. The most critical time in the life of any child is the first eight days; if he survives he will be circumcised on the eighth day. So it was with Israel. Her most critical days were May 14–21, 1948, when thousands of her native sons and daughters were killed and wounded. Even General George C. Marshall said, "There will be no Jews in Israel in six weeks!" Yet the miracle happened and Israel survived.

Bar Mitzvah

The most significant event in the life of a Jewish youth is his *bar mitzvah*. At age thirteen he leaves his childhood behind and assumes some measure of independence. For the young state of Israel, the thirteenth year was 1961; and in that year the nation gained recognition in the eyes of the world in connection with the "Eichmann Affair."

Adolf Eichmann was a henchman of Adolf Hitler and one of the most cruel men who has ever lived. After the war it became known that Eichmann was instrumental in the mass killings of the Jews as well as other peoples during the Nazi reign of terror. He was captured by Israeli officials in South America and taken to Israel to be tried for his crimes. The world was up in arms. There was no judicial precedent that would allow any nation to try criminals for actions which took place before that nation was in existence.

The United Nations had a puzzle on its hands. Eventually, Mrs. Golda Meir, then Israel's UN ambassador, declared that the UN could not censure Israel because the world organization considered Israel an underdeveloped nation. Israel proceeded with the trial of Eichmann and afterward he was electrocuted and his ashes spread over the sea. But a strange thing happened. The United Nations censured Israel for "kidnapping" Eichmann. But by the act of censure it recognized Israel as an equal among the world community of nations. It was a sort of *bar mitzvah* for Israel to be recognized at age thirteen!

A Decade of War, 1967–1977

The third phase in the life of the Jewish male can be designated as the decade of war. Historically, the Israelite man became eligible for service as a soldier at age twenty (see Num. 1:3). When Moses prepared to wage war as the nation encountered its enemies, God told him to number only those men twenty years and older.

Vyndal Jones wrote an essay in 1959 which interpreted some of the prophetic passages. In that paper he said that in 1967 or 1968 a war would sweep the land of Israel. He developed this prophecy in some detail. Many people thought he was jumping to erroneous conclusions, but we all know what happened in 1967. Israel was attacked and the Six Day War ensued just as the nation was reaching its twentieth anniversary. But it was not to be the final war of the decade 1967–1977. In 1973 Israel again went to war after it was attacked on the day of Yom Kippur. In these two wars Israel acquired almost six times as much land as it possessed at its birth.

That decade included some of the most heroic of young Israel's achievements. Can anyone forget the daring Entebbe raid in 1975? A crack Israeli unit flew 2,500 miles, avoided radar, landed in Uganda, killed the terrorists, and freed ninety-one Israeli hostages.

A Decade of Religious Devotion and Peace

The next phase of life for the Jewish man begins at age thirty. It is the period of religious devotion and peace. We recall that Jesus was thirty when He began His ministry. Israel, the "newborn one," reached its thirtieth year in 1978 and began a stage quite obviously characterized by the quest of peace—if not the reality of peace. The nation, which has always had a decidedly religious quality in its character, now has perhaps even more reason for expressing its faith in God given the events unfolded in this decade.

I was in the early stages of writing this book when, in September 1978, the peace accord was signed in Washington, D.C. between Egypt and Israel. Egyptian President Sadat had made his historic trip to Jerusalem in November 1977. Then on March 26, 1979, President Carter hosted Prime Minister Begin and President Sadat in Washington and the peace treaty was signed. It was a tour-de-force in diplomacy.

But even as these things happened, many Jewish leaders began to doubt the United States' commitment to Israel. They wondered if the U.S. would still lend support to Israel if faced with the alternative of losing its supply of oil from the Middle East. Would America be so committed to four million Israelis far from its shores if faced with economic distress for its own 225 million citizens? And what are the prophetic implications of such an event, were it to happen? Could the guarantee of security and military support for Israel constitute the beginning of the seven-year tribulation for the Jews if America abrogated its guarantee halfway into that period? Would the President of the United State emerge as the Antichrist? Time will reveal the answers. I do not know.

Many have asked me, "Anis, why have not the Jews built the temple, now that they have Jerusalem?" Ever since 1967 there have been reports that Israel was assembling materials in order to reconstruct the temple. One persistent rumor was that stones for the temple were being shipped from Indiana or from Rome. Anyone who knows Israel would know such things are entirely without factual foundation. There are enough stones in Palestine to supply the world at a sizable profit. It is not stone that is needed. The *time* is not right. But if our consideration of Israel's "generation" be accurate, sometime within the next few years we can expect Israel to begin rebuilding the temple. That would be the crowning act of her religious life.

Declining Years

A generation is variously measured, but at the most it represents fifty years. At age fifty an Israelite was released from the obligation to serve in the military, or in the temple if he were a priest. His life as an army man or as a public religious figure came to an end. Maturity gave way to the declining years. Now we are living, I believe, in the time of the prophesied generation, "that newborn one." These are some of the most exciting days in the history of the world since the death and resurrection of our Lord. Jesus said that this generation would not pass away until all of these signs are fulfilled.

When Will the World Come to an End?

If our calendar is a correct estimation, then Israel's "newborn one" will reach fifty or "retirement" in the year 1998. But am I saying that Jesus will come then? I certainly am not.

I remind us of the warning of our Lord who said, "But of that day and hour no one knows. . . ." Please do not conclude that "Dr. Anis Shorrosh declares the Lord Jesus is coming in 1998 or the year 2000!" I do not know when and no one else knows. But this we do know. Jesus did say that we can know what signs are to come, and what *sign* is to take place. He answered the disciples' questions not with riddles and mysteries, but with clear answers in understandable language. Time and distance tend to blur the meaning of those words for us and the end of the world may indeed take place before the year 2000. But I must consistently emphasize that no one really knows.

What I am saying is that the coming of our Lord will be very soon. He is coming! The King is coming! The question is, "If the King is coming, what are we as Christians going to do about it?"

Are we wrapped up in this world of materialism? Have we sold our souls to the almighty Dollar? Have we become engrossed with porno movies, drugs, the occult, or anything that makes light of God's Word?

Have we made an idol of the church—or the charismatic movement—or our splendid church music and our great sanctuaries? Are we guilty of setting our eyes on the lowlands rather than on the Lord Jesus Christ? Or are we surrendered to do His will?

In the light of the times in which we live, and because Jesus is coming soon, I suggest to the Christian—rather, I *urge*—that each of us be more careful to spend time with God and His Word. Some church members who consider themselves saved, baptized, sanctified, and pastorized spend more time in one day reading the newspaper or a magazine than they spend reading the Word of God in a month. And then they wonder why they are not mighty giants in the things of the Lord! They are spiritual midgets. Others are "environmental Christians." As long as they are in the church environment they are fine, but when they get away from great preaching and dynamic fellowship they shrink slowly and wither away. Instead of being ruled by our surroundings, we need to be thermostats, regulating the environment wherever we go. God through Jesus Christ has reconciled the world to Himself. As Christians we must allow God to live in us, loving Him, understanding His Word, and sharing His good news.

Some of us who think we are converted are not. I have never seen a country like our United States, where everybody is a member of this or that group—the Moose Club, the Goose Club, the Mickey Mouse Club! But do you belong to Jesus Christ? Being a Christian does not come by any method other than a deep, vital, transforming, and dynamic experience with Jesus Christ. The Holy Spirit will make you aware of the change. As did the people in Ephesus, Christians show forth their deeds, not just their words and a handshake. Christ must be welcomed into your life as your Savior and Lord in sincere, repentant prayer. Then you must totally surrender to Him and obey His will.

The days are upon us. The Rapture is not just a slogan for bumper stickers. It is going to happen very soon. Are you ready?

8

The Rapture —
What A Way To Go!

For if we believe that Jesus died and rose again, even so God will bring with Him those who have fallen asleep in Jesus. For this we say to you by the word of the Lord, that we who are alive, and remain until the coming of the Lord, shall not precede those who have fallen asleep. For the Lord Himself will descend from heaven with a shout, with the voice of the archangel, and with the trumpet of God; and the dead in Christ shall rise first. Then we who are alive and remain shall be caught up together with them in the clouds to meet the Lord in the air, and thus we shall always be with the Lord. Therefore comfort one another with these words.

(1 Thess. 4:14–18)

A few years ago on my arrival in Orlando, Florida, to preach at the First Baptist Church in Pinehills, a huge billboard caught my eye. It was entirely blue except for a little white cloud. Superimposed upon the cloud were the words in large letters—*The Rapture*. Then in smaller letters at the bottom—*What a Way To Go!*

Not too long ago the subject of the Rapture was restricted only to prophetic conferences and to a rather small portion of the church. But today one cannot be among Bible-believing Christians long before someone speaks of it. I believe it is another indication of the "prophecy fever" of which I spoke at the beginning.

But what is the Rapture? If you have tried to find the word in your New Testament you know it is not there. Is the idea biblical? Yes, it is. The word *rapture,* in its prophetic sense, comes from the Latin term used to translate "caught up." It is found in our text: "Then we who are alive and remain shall be *caught up* together with them in the clouds to meet the Lord in the air, and thus we shall always be with the Lord" (v. 17). These words may just as easily be translated "we shall be *raptured.*" The Rapture refers to an experience in time and space when believers who are alive on this earth shall be translated into their glorified bodies to meet the Lord in the air.

Phases of the Rapture

The early Christians looked for the second coming of Christ. Jesus Himself had told them: "In My Father's house are many dwelling places; if it were not so, I would have told you; for I go to prepare a place for you. And if I go and prepare a place for you, I will come again, and receive you to Myself; that where I am, there you may be also" (John 14:2,3).

Paul, in a letter to the church at Corinth, elaborated further on the promised return of Christ. He said, "Behold, I tell you a mystery; we shall not all sleep, but we shall all be changed, in a moment, in the twinkling of an eye, at the last trumpet; for the trumpet will sound, and the dead will be raised imperishable, and we shall be changed" (1 Cor. 15:51,52).

He was telling them that, in light of the imminent return of Christ, not all of them would die (the word "sleep" means to die); all would be changed into gloriously imperishable new creations, but he explains that there would be two groups of believers. Those who had died before Christ's appearance would be resurrected while those who were alive on earth at Christ's coming would be "changed . . . in the twinkling of an eye."

This is essentially what he later wrote to the Thessalonian church. At Christ's coming in the air, the dead believers would first rise to meet Him and those who are alive would be "caught up" or "raptured" to join all believers and be with the Lord forever. This is the blessed hope of Christians alive today. When Christ comes, we who are alive will experience a phenomenal, supernatural, biological transformation at the same instant we defy gravity in our ascension to the great meeting in the air. This is what Hal Lindsey called "the ultimate trip!" I repeat, what a way to go!

We gain insight into what this Rapture will be like as we recall Luke's description of the ascension of Jesus. It is recorded in Acts 1:10,11.

And as they were gazing intently into the sky while He was departing, behold, two men in white clothing stood beside them; and they also said, "Men of Galilee, why do you stand looking into the sky? This Jesus, who has been taken up from you into heaven, will come in just the same way as you have watched Him go into heaven."

When Will the Rapture Take Place?

In my effort to explain the prophetic Scriptures, I acknowledge that sincere believers differ as to the interpretations of these things. Many would even say that there is no such event as a "Rapture," for they see these verses here quoted as pointing to the Second Coming. In this book it is not my intent to refute the views of others, but merely to explain as simply as I know how what the predominant interpretations are and to declare what I believe to be the meaning of the Scriptures.

Among those who believe that the Rapture is a separate,

distinct event from the Second Coming, there are those who hold to a *post-tribulation Rapture*. Agreeing with others that a time of great tribulation (see Matt. 24:21) is coming, they believe that the church will be raptured at the end of the tribulation period. They interpret this to mean that after the seven years of the great tribulation are ended, the Lord Jesus will descend, the dead in Christ will be resurrected, and those who are alive will be raptured and translated, joining Christ who then descends to earth to establish His millennial kingdom.

Another view is what is called the *mid-tribulation Rapture*. According to this view, the church goes through the first three and a half years of the tribulation. Then suddenly at midpoint, when the Antichrist breaks the agreement with Israel, Jesus will appear in the air secretly to His believers, resurrecting those who are dead and snatching away those who are alive. Then begins the terrible, cataclysmic tribulation (see Dan. 9:27) which culminates in the Second Coming. According to this view, Christ returns with His church and believers of all ages to set up His kingdom on earth where He will reign and rule for a thousand years.

Still others espouse a *pre-tribulation Rapture*. I am persuaded that this interpretation is most satisfactory. As its name infers, this interpretation professes that the Rapture will take place before the tribulation begins. Those who advocate this view usually point to several scriptural examples that appear to support such an interpretation.

When God brought judgment on the earth through the Flood He provided a way of escape for Noah and his family (see Gen. 6–8). They also draw attention to the rescuing of Lot out of Sodom and Gomorrah before those wicked cities were destroyed. Although Lot "lingered," God would not allow the destruction of the cities of the plains until Lot was safely out of Sodom (see Gen. 19). A third instance is found in the miraculous deliverance of the children of Israel from Egypt. When

God's judgment began to fall on the land of Egypt, not once were His chosen people ever touched. Neither the Israelites nor their animals were harmed. Even when there was no light in the Egyptian camp, the Bible says that it was daylight in the homes of the Israelites (see Ex. 10:23). The firstborn of the Egyptians were killed; yet the firstborn of the Israelites were spared (see Ex. 12). God reminds us again and again that He preserves us and delivers us from trouble because of His grace.

In addition to these three interpretations, there is what is called the *partial-tribulation Rapture.* According to this view, if one is not spiritual he will be left behind when the Rapture occurs. Those who teach this say that if one has only a head knowledge of theology and not heartfelt faith, the Lord is going to leave him here to go through the tribulation and be purified from his backsliding. I do not know how many people believe this theory, but I question if there is any Scripture that supports it.

Some suggest that this view has arisen out of the charismatic movement. A segment of Christians, it is said, perceive themselves as better than others in the faith. They teach that one who speaks in tongues, heals the sick, or demonstrates other gifts of the Spirit is more spiritual than the rest. I thank God that most charismatics are not guilty of such an attitude.

Billy Graham affirms that "every true Christian is charismatic," with which I agree. Every child of God has the Holy Spirit and is endowed with spiritual gifts. But woe unto any one if he imagines that just because God has given him a gift he is better than anyone else. If anything identifies a Spirit-filled Christian it is *love.* If we are filled with the Spirit, it will be revealed not only by what we say, but how we live. We are judged not only by our orthodox theology, but also by the daily demonstration of our compassion, or the lack of it.

Why the Different Views?

Christians of yesterday and today espouse differing interpretations of the Rapture. Let me emphasize that how we perceive this miracle has nothing to do with our salvation. Being saved does not depend on any particular view of the Rapture. Many born-again Christians prefer the "post-trib" and "mid-trib" positions because they think they see support for these views in Scripture. For instance, some of Jesus' words in the Olivet discourse seem to indicate that we will experience the tribulation. He said, "Unless those days were shortened, no flesh would be saved; but for the elect's sake those days will be shortened" (Matt. 24:22 NKJB–NT). But who are the *elect?* The Jehovah's Witnesses claim they are, pointing to the passage in Revelation 14 which speaks of the 144,000 chosen witnesses on earth in the last times. However, on closer scrutiny it is evident that the 144,000 are in reality Jews from the twelve tribes of Israel (see Rev. 7).

The explanation that appears most satisfactory to me is that the elect are those who know the Lord during the seven-year tribulation. Since God never leaves Himself without a witness, there will be those who come to know Christ and witness for Him even after the church has been raptured. There will be multitudes saved at that time, as Revelation 7:9,14 indicates:

After these things I looked, and behold, a great multitude, which no one could count, from every nation and all tribes and peoples and tongues, standing before the throne and before the Lamb, clothed in white robes, and palm branches were in their hands. . . . And he said to me, "These are the ones who come out of the great tribulation, and they have washed their robes and made them white in the blood of the Lamb."

Need I add anything further? It is for their sake, the elect, that the great tribulation is not too long.

In conclusion, the Rapture is for the Christian the "blessed hope." In that instant we will be snatched away to meet the Lord in the air. Praise the Lord! Some believe it will happen only after the church has experienced the tribulation.

Some believe it will take place in the midst of the seven years. Still others hold that we will be raptured before the tribulation. No one knows. My own personal conviction is that we will be caught up before the tribulation. That could happen at any time. But no matter how we personally view this doctrine, John reminds us that "when He appears, we shall be like Him, because we shall see Him just as He is. And everyone who has this hope *fixed* on Him purifies himself, just as He is pure" (1 John 3:2,3).

9

Who Is the Antichrist?

Now we ask you, brethren, by the coming of our Lord Jesus Christ and our gathering together to Him, that you not be soon shaken in mind or be troubled . . . Let no one deceive you by any means; for that Day will not come unless the falling away comes first, and the man of sin is revealed, the son of perdition, who opposes and exalts himself above all that is called God or that is worshiped, so that he sits as God in the temple of God, showing himself that he is God.

(2 Thess. 2:1–4 NKJB–NT)

Books, magazines, and literature from many Christian organizations and ministries in recent years have reported the existence of a gigantic computer in Brussels, Belgium, capable of computerizing all world trade and assigning a computer number to every human being. Nicknamed "the Beast," Bible prophecy students have expressed the belief that the man who controls this source of information obviously will be a very powerful individual. They have asked, could this be the Antichrist?

I have not been able to track down or verify these reports.

But what we do know is what the Bible tells us concerning the appearance of the Antichrist on the world scene.

Jesus, in His reply to the disciples' questions regarding the sign of His second coming, warned that false christs and false prophets would appear. Then later, in John's epistles to the early church, further warning is issued concerning the Antichrist. John wrote: "This is the antichrist, the one who denies the Father and the Son" (1 John 2:22). John did say that "many antichrists" were already present and doing harm to the church. So as not to be confused, it is necessary to distinguish between these "antichrists" and the one Antichrist.

Anyone who opposes Christ or pretends that he is the Messiah is by definition anti-Christ. These have been with us since the first century. They preach under many different banners—science, humanism, atheistic communism—but they are all antichrists.

Paul's letter to the Thessalonians gives the most revealing disclosure in the New Testament of the Antichrist. In that passage quoted at the beginning of this chapter, he is called the "man of sin" and the "son of perdition." Another revealing prophetic Scripture is Daniel 11:35–45. But the one most often referred to is probably Revelation 13. We will look in vain if we seek the name "Antichrist" in these passages; that term has been adopted to describe the "man of sin," the "son of perdition," or the "beast" of Revelation 13.

And I saw a beast coming up out of the sea, having ten horns and seven heads, and on his horns were ten diadems, and on his heads were blasphemous names. And the beast which I saw was like a leopard, and his feet were like those of a bear, and his mouth like the mouth of a lion. And the dragon gave him his power and his throne and great authority. And I saw one of his heads as if it had been slain, and his fatal wound was healed. And the whole earth was amazed and followed after the beast; and they worshiped the dragon, because he gave his authority to the beast; and they worshiped the beast, saying, "Who is like the beast, and who is able to wage war with him?" And there was given to him a mouth speaking arrogant words

and blasphemies; and authority to act for forty-two months was given
to him. And he opened his mouth in blasphemies against God, to
blaspheme His name and His tabernacle, that is, those who dwell in
heaven. And it was given to him to make war with the saints and to
overcome them; and authority over every tribe and people and tongue
and nation was given to him. And all who dwell on the earth will
worship him, everyone whose name has not been written from the
foundation of the world in the book of life of the Lamb who has been
slain. . . . And he causes all, the small and the great, and the rich
and the poor, and the free men and the slaves, to be given a mark on
their right hand, or on their forehead, and he provides that no one
should be able to buy or to sell, except the one who has the mark,
either the name of the beast or the number of his name. Here is
wisdom. Let him who has understanding calculate the number of the
beast, for the number is that of a man; and his number is six hundred
and sixty-six (Rev. 13:1–8,16–18).

The Significance of Numbers

Before proceeding to discuss the meaning of these passages and the various persons who might fit their description as
the Antichrist, we should note that numbers in the Scriptures
have meaning. Their significance is a factor in recognizing the
Antichrist, for his number will be 666. The numbers whose
values conservative biblical scholars agree upon are these:

One	the absolute unity of the Godhead, Sovereignty
Two	division and trouble
Three	divine completeness
Four	earth, the world
Five	grace
Six	man
Seven	divine perfection
Eight	new beginnings
Nine	judgment
Ten	testimony
Eleven	apostasy
Twelve	the nation Israel
Thirteen	rebellion

Of course, the chapter divisions in the Bible are not inspired, nor were they part of the original manuscripts. But it is a striking coincidence that Revelation 13 is the chapter which describes the political and religious beasts who are the greatest rebels of all time.

Using the table above, it is possible to understand the hideous and prideful meaning of the Antichrist's number. He will be a man, as is plain from the figure six. (Remember, man was created on the sixth day.) The three-fold repetition of the numeral six links the Beast or Antichrist with God and the general understanding is that as a man he claims to be God. This is exactly what Paul says of him:

". . . the son of perdition, who opposes and exalts himself above all that is called God or that is worshiped, so that he sits as God in the temple of God, showing himself that he is God" (2 Thess. 2:3,4 NKJB–NT).

Candidates for the Antichrist

Now let us look at the individuals in history and in our own time who have been thought to be the Antichrist, recognizing as we do that this is not sheer entertainment. The man of sin, more than likely, is alive today and will make his appearance before Christ returns. Let us be prayerfully on the watch.

An Historical Candidate

One of the Seleucid rulers, of that dynasty which succeeded Alexander the Great in the region of Syria and Mesopotamia, bore many of the distinguishing characteristics of the Antichrist. He was Antiochus IV, often called Antiochus Epiphanes. He ruled in Palestine in the second century B.C. So hated was he by his subjects that he was nicknamed Antiochus Epimanes, *Antiochus the Mad*! Coming as he did before Christ, he more aptly fits the description of Daniel's prophecy than he does the New Testament prophecies.

He forbade the worship of Jehovah in the temple in Jerusalem. By erecting a statue of Jupiter Capitolinus as his god in the very center of the temple, he desecrated the temple of God. Further, history documents that in 168 B.C. he brought a sow into the courtyard and sacrificed it on the altar. Then he boiled it and took the broth, sprinkling it over the holy place within the temple. Certainly such atrocities were repulsive and sickening to the Jewish constituency.

Daniel's prophecy says the Antichrist "will show no regard for the gods of his fathers or for the desire of women, nor will he show regard for any other god . . ." (Dan. 11:37). The spiteful treatment of women by Antiochus reached its height when he destroyed the temple of Venus, the goddess of womanhood, at Elymais.

A Biblical Candidate

Only one person in all of Scripture has been called a "devil." That man has been suggested as the Antichrist. Judas Iscariot, one of the twelve disciples of our Lord, was not only called a devil (see John 6:70), he was also pointed out as "the son of perdition" (John 17:12 KJV) which matches another of the Antichrist's names in 2 Thessalonians 2:3. *Perdition* is a word that is little used now; it had the connotation of eternal damnation, the future misery of the wicked, utter destruction, and ruin. It is synonymous with the term "son of hell" used by Jesus (see Matt. 23:15).

Anyone who would believe that the Antichrist and Judas Iscariot are one and the same would have to believe that Judas would make some kind of reincarnational appearance, a return trip to earth. But the prophecy recorded in Revelation 13:3 seems to make allowance for something like that when it says that John saw the Beast's "fatal wound" and it was healed.

Judas died instantaneously, but nothing in the account of his life suggests a supernatural reappearance.

A Political Candidate

Several of the emperors of the Roman Empire have seemed to fit the description of the Antichrist, and one can easily imagine that first century Christians ''knew'' that the emperor was the Antichrist. Diocletian and Hadrian seem to be candidates, but no one stands out among the Roman rulers as does Caesar Augustus Nero. He ruled Rome A.D. 54–68.

It is said that he fiddled while Rome burned. Historians do not discount the possibility that Nero had his own men set fire to the city. Wanting a renovated Rome, the neurotic Nero could have thought he would accomplish two things at once—burn the old city and kill all the Christians to rid the state of their growing influence. A terrifying persecution took place in A.D. 65 and at that time it is thought the greatest missionary who ever lived, the apostle Paul, was beheaded.

Nero's name, according to the numbers of the Hebrew alphabet, is calculated at 666. And he did die of a wound; he committed suicide by falling upon his own sword. However, he did not come back to life.

Religious Candidates

In the fourteenth century Pope Paul the Innocent pointed out to the world the man whom he believed to be the Antichrist—the prophet Muhammad. I did not know of the pope's action until recently, but I have long believed that Muhammad may have been (and may become) the Antichrist.

The founder of the Muslim religion, Muhammad (507?–632) has had an influence over more of humanity than do most men. Today some 600 million people follow Islam. They do not revere Muhammad as God, but as the prophet of Allah, and they believe a little of the truth concerning Jesus—enough to immunize them against the true Christ who is the Way, the Truth, and the Life!

The Koran, the holy book of Islam, is smaller than the New Testament. In it is a summary of the Old and New Testaments put together by the prophet. It contains gross mistakes. Miriam, the sister of Moses, is said to be Miriam, the mother of Jesus. Judas was crucified, not Jesus. The prophet believed that "prophet Jesus" was too good to be killed and that rather than dying, Jesus went straight to heaven. Muhammad was convinced that Christians are "shirkers," believers in more than one God. Faith in a triune God is not acceptable in Islam.

Muhammad also affirmed that the divinity of Jesus Christ was a heresy, the result of the Christians' overemphasis of the goodness of Christ. On this central doctrine, the Muslims misunderstand biblical truth. Jesus is not God in the sense that He was a great man who eventually achieved divinity. It is the other way around. God is Jesus. Thus, the divine God became man, for man can never become God. When one understands this, he has achieved much in comprehending the nature of the divinity of Jesus.

At different times, the Roman Catholic pope has been thought to be the Antichrist. In fact, no other personage has been so frequently identified with the Antichrist as has the pope. Those who believe this point to the following similarities between the pope and Antichrist:

1. The prophecy (see Dan. 11:36) says he (the Antichrist) will do according to his will. The pope is not responsible to any earthly authority.

2. The pope considers himself above civil rulers who call themselves gods. The Emperor of Japan and other lesser figures have been considered divine for many years. Even now an attempt is being made to restore that title to the Emperor

after a lapse of more than thirty years. It is said of the Antichrist "'he will exalt and magnify himself above every god . . .'" (Dan. 11:36). When a pope is enthroned, the church hierarchy recite Psalm 95, which actually refers to the Lord Jesus Christ.

3. The Antichrist will consider himself above the Word of God. In the Catholic church, papal encyclicals are equally authoritative as Scripture.

4. Heathenism is incorporated in the worship of the Roman Catholic Church. To signify consecration, holy water is sprinkled over objects and people, a practice not unlike what goes on in Buddhist and Hindu temples. The title of the pope itself, *pontiff,* is borrowed from the ancient Roman *pontific,* a title used by the high priest in ancient Rome's heathen religions.

5. The Antichrist is not expected to have a normal regard for women, as stated in Daniel 11:37. The centuries-old practice of mandatory celibacy in the Catholic church is, of course, contrary to Scripture (see 1 Tim. 4:3).

6. The Antichrist, Daniel 11:38 declares, "will honor a god of fortresses," or a "god protector." Catholics venerate the Virgin Mary and many saints as their protectors. The pope and his college of cardinals have for centuries assigned "sainthood" to any individual deemed worthy. Thus the pope becomes a "saint protector" or a "god protector." Since only God is deserving of adoration and prayer, these saints in a sense are lesser gods.

7. The man of sin is also to be in control of gold, silver, and precious stones (see Dan. 11:38). Again, the pope fulfills this description; the Roman Catholic church is actually the richest organization in the world, controlling more gold, silver, precious stones, and valuable relics than any person or most nations.

8. Lastly, this person, according to Daniel 11:39, is to divide the land. Across the centuries, the choicest lands have been acquired by the Catholic church.

This is an impressive enough list that many Christians think they can identify the pope as the Antichrist. But I ask, if the pope is truly the Antichrist, why has not Jesus, the true Messiah, appeared? I do not see how we can make the identification without the Second Coming.

Modern Candidates

Few men in any century fit the description of "beast" as did Adolf Hitler, Germany's dictator and warlord. Hitler is accountable to a large degree for the twenty million war deaths between 1939 and 1945. In addition, his persecution and attempted extermination of the Jews has never been equalled in the annals of civilization. Three to six million Jews lost their lives in the torture chambers, concentration camps, and gas chambers as he and his Nazi troops sought to put into effect the "final solution" of the Jewish problem. Thank God that His chosen people survived the Holocaust and are today rebuilding their own land. But had not God cut him short, Hitler most surely would have wiped them from the earth.

During the war years it was common to hear the name Adolf Hitler associated with the Beast of Revelation 13. As the war ended and the facts of the Soviet purge came to light, another name began to be mentioned, that of Joseph Stalin. He was also a mass killer, fitting the description of the Beast in Revelation 13:15. Robert Conquest in his book, *The Great Terror,* documented at least twenty million deaths and attributed them to Stalin. Stalin's own death was a horrible thing. His daughter, Svetlana Aliluyeva, describes his chilling, awful end in the first letter of her book *Twenty Letters to a Friend.*[1] The book also reveals how tormented his life was. Certainly if neither Hitler nor Stalin prove to be the Antichrist, one cannot even imagine how evil and inhuman the true Antichrist will be!

His name should not be mentioned in such close association with Hitler and Stalin, but President John F. Kennedy was thought by some to be the Antichrist. No leader in America in the last several decades so captured the hearts of the people as did Kennedy—and not just the hearts of Americans alone, but of the whole world. When he was assassinated in Dallas in November 1963, some people held so tenaciously to their conviction that Kennedy was the Antichrist that they fully expected him to recover from his "fatal wound" and come up out of his casket alive.

I believe that only a few extremists really felt Kennedy was the Antichrist, but some students of biblical prophecy are wondering if former Secretary of State Henry Kissinger is the man.

Henry Kissinger's name, when translated into Hebrew, has a numerical value of 111 which, of course, is 666 when multiplied by the number of man. Is that a mere coincidence? Many people are convinced that Kissinger is the Antichrist because he is a Jew. They say that because *christ* means "anointed one" or Messiah, the Jews will be looking for one of their own to be the Messiah. Only a Jew would be acceptable to them. To a large number of people, given the gathered facts—and especially because he is Jewish—the identity of the Antichrist is clear. They believe that Kissinger will make a comeback in world politics, a course of events which is quite possible.

But not everyone is convinced about Kissinger. Another prominent person suggested by some was Moshe Dayan, the celebrated hero of the Jews' Six Day War of victory against Egypt and her Arab allies. The striking appearance of the man, the fact that he lost one eye in battle (a sort of "fatal wound"), added to the mystery surrounded him. It is true, normally, that if a bullet were to strike a person in the eye he would die instantly. But Mr. Dayan recovered and the wound was healed. Prophecy students who regarded Dayan as the false messiah predicted that he would become Israel's prime minister. However, he died in 1981.

One other contemporary whose name is raised in discussions of the identity of the Antichrist is the Korean religious leader, Sun Myung Moon. Recently a rabbi in White Plains, New York compared Moon's Unification Church with the Nazi youth movement and the infamous People's Temple of Guyana.

Sun Myung Moon was born Yong Myung Moon (which means Dragon Shining Moon) on January 6, 1920, the second son of eight children. His father, a farmer, was a member of the Presbyterian church in Kwanglu Sangsa Ri in North Korea. Moon received his high school education in Seoul in a Pentecostal school that evidently influenced him greatly as a youth. As a sixteen-year-old, Moon claims, Jesus appeared to him while he was praying and told him he was chosen to finish the work begun by Jesus. Since many underground Pentecostals were expecting a Korean messiah, Moon announced his calling.

During World War II Moon attended Waseda University in Tokyo, studying electrical engineering. He returned to Korea in 1944 and gathered some followers. Four years later, however, the Presbyterian Church in Korea excommunicated him. He had become affiliated with a Paik Moon Kim who publicly declared that Moon fulfilled the Korean expectations of a messiah. This Moon did not deny. And at the same time he was establishing his Broad Sea Church and publishing the *Divine Principle,* an account of Moon's ''revelations'' that were to become the essence of the Unification Church doctrine.

From 1946 to 1950 Moon claims he was in prison for anti-communist activities. Reportedly, the charge really was adultery and bigamy. In 1954 his wife of ten years left him. In 1960 he married 18-year-old Han Hak Ja, claiming it was his second marriage, but he is accused of being married a total of four times. Han Hak Ja has borne him eight children.

In the early '50s Moon established a following in Pusan and in 1954 officially launched the Holy Spirit Association for the Unification of World Christianity—termed the Unification Church for short. The complete *Divine Principle* was published three years later, which Moon claimed was the new revelation from God. It was revised in 1966 and released that year in the United States.

When Moon married Han Hak Ja, his followers considered it the marriage of the Lamb, a sign of Messiahship in the *Divine Principle*. This was considered to be the union of two "perfect" people and the beginning of a movement toward a perfect world, the kingdom of heaven on earth.

Moon says that God told him in January 1972 to go to America and he obeyed. As quoted four years later by *Time,* his goal is to spread the "truth" of his *Divine Principle* throughout the nations: "Once our movement arouses the interest of the people in a nation, through mass media it will spread throughout the world. . . . So, we are going to focus our attention on one nation from where to reach the world. . . ." [2] His organization has been embroiled in controversy in America, partly because of his alleged connections with Korean politicians and his wealth. His estate is estimated to be worth approximately $1 million and his net financial worth is reportedly more than $15 million. Moon insists that he is the "third Adam" and the real Christ.

The Shape of Things to Come

God has seen fit to veil the identity of the coming Beast whose number is 666. No one knows who the Antichrist is at this time, but I repeat the solemn truth. If indeed we are living in the last generation before Christ's coming—and many Christians believe that we are—then the Antichrist is almost certainly alive somewhere on earth today.

Another scenario is presented by some, based upon the presumption that the Antichrist will turn out to be the director of the European Common Market. They envision a leader making a treaty of economic and military aid with Israel following the Rapture. Then, halfway into a seven-year period, he will break the agreement as pressure is applied by OPEC (the Organization of Petroleum Exporting Countries). OPEC, whose membership is dominated by Middle Eastern Arab nations, will demand that Western European nations back off from their support of Israel—and allow the occupied territories in Palestine to return to the Arabs—or they will cut off the vital oil supply.

Others say that the United States, not the Common Market, will be the friend who will make a peace treaty with Israel, and then become Israel's foe as the OPEC nations apply pressure over the availability of oil. (Would this indicate that the U.S. president would turn out to be the Antichrist? I heartily hope not!) Those holding this view say that the American government will decide it must give up its steady support of 4 million Israelis, 7000 miles away, rather than allowing economic chaos and deprivation to plague its own 225 million citizens.

In either case, it is not hard to imagine such an event taking place. We saw what chaos and high prices the 1973 oil embargo caused. In a new situation, Israel might well be caught in the middle without support from her friends. There would be only one direction for her to turn:

And it will come about in that day that I will set about to destroy all the nations that come against Jerusalem. And I will pour out on the house of David and on the inhabitants of Jerusalem, the Spirit of grace and of supplication, so that they will look on Me whom they have pierced; and they will mourn for Him, as one mourns for an only son, and they will weep bitterly over Him, like the bitter weeping over a first-born (Zech. 12:9,10).

Israel will then, at last, be ready to embrace the coming Messiah who, after the destruction of the Beast, will establish His kingdom for a millennium on earth.

10

The Seventieth Week of Daniel

Now while I was speaking and praying, and confessing my sin and the sin of my people Israel, and presenting my supplication before the LORD my God in behalf of the holy mountain of my God, while I was still speaking in prayer, then the man Gabriel, whom I had seen in the vision previously, came to me in my extreme weariness about the time of the evening offering. And he gave me instruction and talked with me, and said, "O Daniel, I have now come forth to give you insight with understanding. At the beginning of your supplications the command was issued, and I have come to tell you, for you are highly esteemed; so give heed to the message and gain understanding of the vision. Seventy weeks have been decreed for your people and your holy city, to finish the transgression, to make an end of sin, to make atonement for iniquity, to bring in everlasting righteousness, to seal up vision and prophecy, and to anoint the most holy place. So you are to know and discern that from the issuing of a decree to restore and rebuild Jerusalem until Messiah the Prince there will be seven weeks and sixty-two weeks; it will be built again, with plaza and moat, even in times of distress. Then after the sixty-two weeks the Messiah will be cut off and have nothing, and the people of the prince who is to come will destroy the city and the sanctuary. And its end will come with a flood; even to the end there will be war; desolations are determined. And he will make a firm covenant with the many for one week, but in the middle of the week he will put a stop to sacrifice and grain offering; and on the wing of abominations will come one who makes desolate, even until a complete destruction, one that is decreed, is poured out on the one who makes desolate."

(Dan. 9:20–27)

For any Jew who tries to arrive at a specific interpretation of the chronology of this prophectic passage, there is still an ancient curse: "May his bones and his memory rot who shall attempt to number the seventy weeks." We acknowledge that there are difficulties with the passage, along with differing interpretations, but we should not be discouraged thereby from seeking to comprehend this vital prophecy.

Daniel's Discovery

Jeremiah, the prophet of God who lived in the seventh century B.C. in Jerusalem, was truly a remarkable seer. He predicted accurately the downfall of Judah and its subsequent captivity by the Babylonians (see Jer. 25:11,12; 29:10–14). Approximately seventy years later, as one of those who were suffering the exile in Babylon, Daniel understood what his predecessor Jeremiah had said.

. . . I, Daniel, observed in the books the number of the years which was revealed as the word of the LORD to Jeremiah the prophet for the completion of the desolations of Jerusalem, namely, seventy years (Dan. 9:2).

Daniel then received a remarkable revelation of prophecy while in an extended period of prayer. W. A. Criswell says of this prayer (vv. 4–19) that it is "the finest example of prayer in the Old Testament. Daniel pours out his heart to God in confession for the sins of Israel and proclaims God as wholly righteous. . . . Daniel intercedes in earnest petition for the restoration of the nation in the land of God's promise.''[1] One cannot help but conclude that it was Daniel's fervent intercession that opened the way for him to receive the revelation. Gabriel the archangel revealed to him a vision of an historical nature stretching over a period of ''seventy weeks.''

Practically every biblical scholar agrees that the seventy weeks of Daniel 9 are in reality coded as weeks of years, not days. In other words, the seventy weeks represent weeks of seven years each, or 490 years total. In Genesis 41, in Joseph's interpretation of Pharaoh's dream, we see an example of the use of seven in this manner. ''The seven good cows are seven years; and the seven good ears are seven years . . .'' (41:26). The Hebrew word for seven, *shabua,* like our English word does not carry with it a connotation of seven days or seven years. It merely means seven. Daniel prayed about years; yet he was answered in terms of periods of years. Thus, ''seven weeks'' (v. 25) would be 49 years and ''sixty-two weeks'' would be 434 years. Added together they comprise 483 years and when joined with the seventieth week (v. 27) the total is 490 years.

Daniel's vision must have been given him in the year 538 B.C., near the close of the Babylonian exile. Evidently he figured the beginning of the seventy years from the year when he himself was taken captive, in 606 B.C. The vision took place at ''the time of the evening offering,'' which would be at approximately three o'clock. It is relatively easy to determine that, but the essential question is, of course, when did this 490-year period begin?

According to verse 25, the seventy weeks are to be reckoned from a point in time when a decree was given to ''restore and rebuild Jerusalem.'' Four such decrees were issued, one of which must be the one that fits Daniel's prophecy.

1. Cyrus' decree, 539 B.C. (Ezra 6:1,14; Is. 44:28).
2. Darius Hystapis' decree, 519 B.C. (Ezra 6:12).
3. Artaxerxes' decree, 457 B.C. (Ezra 7:13–26).
4. Artaxerxes' second decree, 445 B.C. (Neh. 2:1,7).

The vision of the 490 years has been interpreted in three major ways.

An Historical Interpretation

Antiochus IV, Epiphanes, whom we discussed in the previous chapter, is thought by many to be the one man in history to whom Daniel's words apply. He did stop the sacrifices in Jerusalem by decree and persecuted the Jews fiercely. Moreover, he erected a statue to his god in the temple and demanded that the Jews sacrifice and worship the marble statue of Jupiter. But on closer scrutiny it is clear that Antiochus IV does not meet all of the requirements of the prophecy. He neither left the sanctuary and the city in ruins nor did his date of arrival on the horizon of history coincide with the prophetic calendar. He missed the date by two centuries.

Onias III, a Jewish high priest during the second century B.C., is considered by some to be the Messiah who is "cut off" (v. 26). He was murdered in 171 B.C. But the date of his death misses the timetable of the 490 years by more than a century. Counting back from 171 B.C. we arrive at a date far earlier than Cyrus' decree, the earliest of the four under consideration. Alexander the Great, whose name has also been suggested as the "anointed one cut off," cannot be seriously considered. He died in 323 B.C.

Darius' decree was more properly a reaffirmation of the command of Cyrus. Both of these earlier decrees must be dismissed in any historical interpretation. Figuring 490 years from the decree of Cyrus in 539 B.C. leads us to 49 B.C., a date for which history records no significant events that in any way fulfill Daniel's prophecy.

The Biblical Interpretation—Jesus Himself Fulfilled It

King Artaxerxes declared his intention to rebuild Jerusalem in 457 B.C. Forty-nine years later, in 408 B.C., the project was completed. Therefore the first period of the seventy weeks—the "seven weeks" (v. 25) or 49 years—is fulfilled.

But what of the second block of time, the "sixty-two weeks"? (For ease of understanding, this will be referred to as 434 years.) By taking 434 from 408, the year the rebuilding was accomplished, we have the year A.D. 27, the approximate year in which Jesus of Nazareth began his public ministry as "the Messiah, the Prince." Matthew 3:13–17 tells of the baptism of Jesus and his anointing with the Spirit. The word "Messiah," we know, means "anointed one." Andrew excitedly told his brother Simon ". . . we have found the Messiah" (John 1:41).

Part of the difficulty in interpreting verse 27 stems from the indefinite pronoun "he." Is it referring to the Messiah or to the "prince who is to come" (v. 26)?

In verse 27 we read that "he will make a firm covenant with the many for one week, but in the middle of the week he will put a stop to sacrifice and grain offering. . . ." Jesus, it is believed, confirmed God's everlasting covenant for three and a half years. First, he demonstrated this confirmation by His teaching and preaching and then ratified it by His death, which brought an end to the entire sacrificial system established by Moses and the Old Testament. A "new testament" is now in effect. The elaborate sacrificial system was a shadow of what is to come (see Col. 2:17). Jesus was the fulfillment and substance of that type of shadow.

This interpretation further argues that Jesus was crucified—"cut off"—in the midst of the seventieth week, A.D. 31. Naturally, one must ask, "What about the remaining three and one half years?"

Those who adhere to this interpretation declare that the preaching of the gospel of grace in Jerusalem brought multitudes to the Lord. Alarmed, the Jewish leaders called the gifted preacher Stephen before the Council. His remarkable defense of his faith is one of the high water marks of the New Testament record. When the Council rejected Stephen's testimony, Stephen accused them of resisting the Holy Spirit and rejecting the Messiah who alone could bring their nation salvation. In a fury of hate, the Sanhedrin snatched Stephen, led him out of the city, and stoned him. Thus Stephen became the first Christian martyr. As nearly as we can calculate, this tragic event took place in A.D. 34. This singular event terminated the 490 years allotted to the Jewish nation. The "seventy weeks" could be called "the times of the Jews."

According to this interpretation, the rejection of the Messiah by the Jews and the subsequent stoning of Stephen inaugurated the "times of the Gentiles." They quote Jesus, who said, ". . . and Jerusalem will be trampled by the Gentiles until the times of the Gentiles are fulfilled" (Luke 21:24 NKJB–NT). Indeed, when so few Jews accepted Christ and the majority of them bitterly opposed Paul and Barnabas while the Gentiles did embrace Jesus as Savior, Paul announced: "Since you repudiate it, and judge yourselves unworthy of eternal life, behold, we are turning to the Gentiles" (Acts 13:46). And again in Acts 18:6, Paul "shook out his garments and said to them [Jews], 'Your blood be upon your own heads! I am clean. From now on I shall go to the Gentiles.' " A number of students of prophecy believe that the death of Stephen or the destruction of Jerusalem in A.D. 70 by Titus and the Roman forces signaled the beginning of the times of the Gentiles. Furthermore it is affirmed that 1967 was the year which indicated the end of these times since in that year the Jews regained possession of the entire city of Jerusalem. I have no argument with those who hold to these interpretations of the "times of the Gentiles," but the so-called biblical interpretation of Daniel's seventieth week will be seen to have at least two fatal flaws.

First, the indefinite pronoun "he" in verse 27 and "the

prince'' in verse 26 cannot be Christ. Neither Jesus nor His followers destroyed Jerusalem and the temple. Second, a fundamental fact emerges. Jesus did not make a covenant for one week with anyone, as verse 27 states concerning ''the prince.'' Jesus the Christ made an everlasting covenant of grace and salvation with everyone who will believe in Him.

The Prophecy Is To Be Fulfilled Eschatologically

Still a third interpretation may be most satisfactory. It predicts the events of the seventy weeks as having both an historical and an eschatological fulfillment.

This interpretation dates the ''issuing of a decree'' from 444 B.C. when Artaxerxes commanded that Jerusalem be restored (see Neh. 2:1–8). By moving forward to A.D. 33, the year many suggest as the date of Jesus' crucifixion, we calculate that 477 years would transpire. Immediately we see that this is not in agreement with the 483 years (the 69 years of Daniel's vision; the seventieth week must be interpreted separately). But this is because we are figuring on the basis of our solar year. The Jews and Babylonians reckoned time by using a lunar year of 360 days. When we adjust for this difference and allow one year for the transition from A.D. to B.C., we come very close to the year A.D. 33, the year when Jesus the Messiah was cut off.

The Roman general Titus may indeed fulfill the prophecy of verse 26, but that which the following verse states cannot be true of him. With this and what we have said above, I am convinced that the whole passage refers to none other than a future Antichrist. This ungodly prince will actually impose upon the Jewish people an unyielding agreement demanding that they follow him as their god. Paul referred to this man as

. . . the man of lawlessness is revealed the son of destruction, who opposes and exalts himself above every so-called god or object of worship, so that he takes his seat in the temple of God, displaying himself as being God (2 Thess. 2:3,4).

Because the agreement is made with "the many" (v. 27), it seems likely that this refers to the many Jews who will succumb in the last days and become subservient to the Antichrist. The expression allows also for the fact that not *all* Jews will worship this false Messiah. Note also that he will not be the one who destroys Jerusalem; that will be done by "his people."

The Antichrist will break the agreement "in the middle of the week," thus fulfilling Daniel 12:11 and 2 Thessalonians 2:3,4. The entire church age falls between the sixty-ninth week, after the death of the Messiah, and the "little horn" described in the seventh chapter of Daniel.

The final three and a half years of the seventieth week are described in verse 27. This span of time seems identical with the hour of temptation referred to in Revelation 3:10, the time of trouble mentioned in Daniel 12:1, and the great tribulation of Matthew 24:15–28.

Daniel says that "on the wing of abominations will come one who makes desolate. . . ." The term "abominations" can mean horrible things or abominable idolatries. When Jesus used this verse, we read it in large letters, "ABOMINATION OF DESOLATION" (Mark 13:14). The Septuagint and the Vulgate translations agree on a literal reading of this significant passage as follows: "Upon the temple shall come the abominations of desolation."

Comparing Revelation 13:15 with Daniel's prophecy, it becomes obvious that the Antichrist's image in the temple at Jerusalem is actually the horrible thing or the abominable idol. True, Antiochus Epiphanes did erect a statue of his god, Jupiter Capitolinus, in the temple in 168 B.C. and he did offer a sow upon the altar. But neither bore his own image.

Consequently, it seems to me that the Antichrist is yet to come and that the Rapture will take place before His arrival. The earth's people will apparently agree to the Antichrist's control and rule. Those who do not accept the mark will be killed. I am convinced that the terrifying tribulation is intended for the Jews, specifically, and for the Gentile unbelieving world in general. However, the Rapture is also meant to rescue God's own before the diabolical, destructive, and despicable character arrives on the horizon of a selfish, self-righteous, and faint-hearted world. The accuracy of Daniel's prophecy influenced multitudes of Jews of his generation to be saved.

11
The Three Armageddons

And they gathered them together to the place called in Hebrew, Armageddon.

(Rev. 16:16 NKJB–NT)

When I was a boy growing up in Nazareth, one of our favorite trips was a visit to the plain of Megiddo. The major produce in the valley was wheat and I still remember the beauty of those golden grain fields. For miles and miles the wheat spread before the eyes like a golden-hued ocean. Today wheat is still grown there in abundance. But other crops have also been introduced: apples, bananas, radishes, onions, oranges, lemons—even cotton.

For centuries the plain of Megiddo or Jezreel, as the region also is known, has been the breadbasket of Palestine along with the Jordan Valley. It takes its name from the ancient city of Megiddo.

The ominous word *Armageddon* is associated geographically with this very area. It is here that the final great battle of history, the war to end all wars, is to be fought. Actually this significance is contained in the very name Armageddon, which means literally "hill of slaughter" or "hill of the cut off."

Historical Facts

Megiddo is first mentioned in Scripture in Judges 5:19, the famed "Song of Deborah." The prophetess Deborah, aided by Barak, had just vanquished the forces of Canaan led by Sisera and exclaimed: "The kings came and fought;/Then fought the kings of Canaan/At Taanach near the waters of Megiddo;/They took no plunder in silver./The stars fought from heaven,/From their courses they fought against Sisera" (5:19,20).

Israel's very wicked King Ahab engaged the Syrian armies on the plain of Megiddo and it was there he lost his life as the prophet Micaiah said he would (see 1 Kings 22).

A natural battlefield, it has been the site of major battles throughout history. According to Hal Lindsey, the emperor Napoleon is said to have stood "upon the hill of Megiddo and recalled prophecy as he looked over the valley and said '. . . all the armies of the world could maneuver for battle here.' "[1] From its northernmost point not far from modern Haifa, the plain measures some twenty miles long and fourteen miles across. The British General Allenby defeated the Turks here in October 1918, earning for himself the title of Earl of Megiddo.

The War of Armageddon

The fighting foretold in prophecy that is to take place on the plain of Megiddo is described in Ezekiel 37–39 and in Revelation 16. If I understand these Scriptures correctly, three battles are indicated. Armageddon will not be a single battle; rather it will be the War of Armageddon.

Ezekiel 37 deals with the restoration of Israel to the land. Here is found the well known "dry bones" passage in which Ezekiel is commanded by the Lord to prophesy to the dry bones. This biblical passage is not material for revival preaching only; it is fundamentally a prophecy concerning Israel as a nation. Her spiritual restoration is to come later—here the survival and revival of the nation is the first concern.

Note her condition as described in verse 11:

Then He said to me, "Son of man, these bones are the whole house of Israel; behold, they say, 'Our bones are dried up, and our hope has perished. We are completely cut off.' "

Was the Jewish nation ever in a more desolate state than she was after World War II? The world will never forget what Hitler did to the Jews. When the Allied forces liberated Germany and Poland they found only a few Jewish survivors, most of them in concentration camps. I have visited the museum near the Hill of Zion in Jerusalem and seen there what despicable and diabolical things were done to the Jews during the last war. I wept, wondering how human beings could be so debased toward their own kind when again I saw the same thing during our summer pilgrimage to the Holy Land and Europe in June 1980. We visited the Mauthausen concentration camp near Vienna, Austria, where 90,000 were killed.

But Ezekiel prophesied a future salvation from such deaths as the Jews endured in the Holocaust. "And I will put My Spirit within you, and you will come to life, and I will place you on your own land. Then you will know that I, the LORD, have spoken and done it, declares the Lord" (v. 14).

As an Arab who loves the Lord Jesus, I can tell you this prophecy has been fulfilled today. Most Arabs neither know nor believe such prophecies, but they are in the Bible so that we can know that the Lord keeps His word. In verse 21 the promise of Israel's return is made even more explicit:

And say to them, "Thus says the Lord GOD, 'Behold, I will take the sons of Israel from among the nations where they have gone, and I will gather them from every side and bring them into their own land.' "

There is an interesting comment made in this passage regarding the restored nation's military might. When Ezekiel prophesied to the dry bones, "breath came into them, and they came to life, and stood on their feet, an exceedingly great army" (v. 10). Little Israel is among the most powerful of military forces in the world today. In twenty-four hours the nation can mobilize a militia of practically one million men and women!

The First Battle of Armageddon

With Israel dwelling securely in the land in the last days, the stage will be set for Armageddon. Ezekiel 38 deals with the first battle of Megiddo.

"And the word of the LORD came to me saying, 'Son of man, set your face toward Gog of the land of Magog, the prince of Rosh, Meshech, and Tubal, and prophesy against him' " (vv. 1,2).

It is believed that "Gog" is a reference to modern Russia. One leading biblical scholar earlier in this century, in writing explanatory notes to this passage, remarks: "That the primary reference is to the northern (European) powers, headed up by Russia, all agree." [2] Conservative Old Testament scholars have suggested that "Meshech" is Moscow and "Tubal" is the city of Tobolsk. Later in the passage, the Lord says He will draw Gog "out of the remote parts of the north," a fact agreeing completely with the geographical relationship of Moscow and Israel. The Russian capital is due north of Jerusalem.

We find in verses 3–6 that the first battle involves a coalition of the forces of North Africa, Western Asia, and Russia:

And say, "Thus says the Lord God, 'Behold, I am against you, O Gog, prince of Rosh, Meshech, and Tubal. And I will turn you about, and put hooks into your jaws, and I will bring you out, and all your army, horses and horsemen, all of them splendidly attired, a great company with buckler and shield, all of them wielding swords; Persia, Ethiopia, and Put with them, all of them with shield and helmet; Gomer with all its troops; Beth-togarmah from the remote parts of the north with all its troops—many peoples with you.' "

The next two verses indicate what will happen and what is the destination of these assembled forces.

" 'Be prepared, and prepare yourself, you and all your companies that are assembled about you, and be a guard for them. After many days you will be summoned; in the latter years you will come into the land that is restored from the sword, whose inhabitants have been gathered from many nations to the mountains of Israel which had been a continual waste; but its people were brought out from the nations, and they are living securely, all of them.' "

Note the phrases "after many days" and "in the latter years." Such expressions are repeated often and are quite significant. Ezekiel prophesied approximately six centuries before Christ. Today, 2,600 years afterward, the land of Palestine is partially restored "from the sword" and her inhabitants have literally been "gathered" from all over the world. Even the reference to the land having been "a continual waste" fits perfectly with what we know of Palestine. It is blossoming as the rose, alive with produce and mineral industries. Surely its prosperity adds to its allure as a prize for the forces of Gog.

But of course the prize in the Middle East is oil. Even though the forces of Gog have an ample supply now (Russia is said to have the world's greatest oil reserves), it is only a matter of time before that supply is depleted. Russia could well be biding her time until the circumstances are right for her to move directly into the Persian Gulf region and secure not only a supply of oil but strategic warm water ocean ports as well.

Developments in Iran show how quickly the delicate balance of power is changing in the Middle East. While the Shah was in power, Iran posed no military threat to Israel even though Iran supported the cause of the Palestinian Arabs against Israel. Iran sold oil to Israel and even exchanged diplomats at the consular level. But with a fanatical Islamic government ruling Iran, any observer can see the handwriting on the wall. Ezekiel's prophecy of a coalition of forces may coincide with what is prophesied of "the kings from the east" (Rev. 16:12) who are to figure in the first battle of Armageddon. The entire Muslim world supports the Palestinian Arabs in their claim to Palestine, a claim which Israel refuses to acknowledge. Could Iran and Iraq be the "kings of the east" who will descend with Syria, Jordan, Libya, Ethiopia, and Saudi Arabia upon Israel?

Or is "the kings of the east" a reference to China as Hal Lindsey and others believe? The forces of Gog could come down upon Israel only to be attacked by the Chinese army.

We can determine from this passage in Ezekiel 38 that *the first battle of Armageddon will not take place any time soon.*

First, the nation Israel is spoken of as "living securely" in the land. Verse 11 says that Israel's cities will be "without walls . . . having no bars or gates. . . ." One does not have to travel to Palestine to know that Israel does not enjoy that kind of security. There must be peace between Arab and Jew before Israel can feel secure. Now Israel does not only have bars and gates; electronic surveillance equipment monitors countless buildings and ports of entry, and land mines dot its borders. There is no peace.

Further, Armageddon is apparently years away because the prophecy says that Gog will come to plunder Israel when she has "acquired cattle and goods" (v. 12). Until recently

Israel had very few cattle. Approximately ten years ago an Arizona cattleman brought a herd of beautiful heifers to Israel. They are now being raised in the Golan Heights and I have seen them there. Before long, Israel will be a land of cattle.

Whenever the first battle of Armageddon breaks out, it is clear from this passage that the Lord will fight for Israel. Verse 19 declares that "in My zeal and in My blazing wrath I declare that on that day there will surely be a great earthquake in the land of Israel." Some students of prophecy conjecture that what follows is a description of thermonuclear war. Israel is believed to have the capacity to wage war with nuclear weapons, as does Russia. Of course, the meaning of verse 20 may refer to the earthquake:

"And the fish of the sea, the birds of the heavens, the beasts of the field, all the creeping things that creep on the earth, and all the men who are on the face of the earth will shake at My presence; the mountains also will be thrown down, the steep pathways will collapse, and every wall will fall to the ground.

The Second Battle

Chapter 39, I believe, describes a second battle. Apparently there is a regrouping of forces, perhaps within the seven-year tribulation. I see these two battles taking place, one at the outset of the great tribulation of seven years and the second at the end of the seven years.

"And you, son of man, prophesy against Gog, and say, 'Thus says the Lord GOD, "Behold I am against you, O Gog, prince of Rosh, Meshech, and Tubal: and I shall turn you around, drive you on, take you up from the remotest parts of the north, and bring you against the mountains of Israel' " (vv. 1,2).

Apparently most of Russia's allies will have been defeated in the first battle. But Russia is still strong. She and "the peoples who are with" her will come again against Israel.

"And I shall strike your bow from your left hand, and dash down your arrows from your right hand" (v. 3).

It is possible that after the two battles all sophisticated military armament and materials will have been eliminated. In other words, world disarmament could become a reality between the first and second battles since this prophecy speaks of primitive, conventional weapons only.

In the next three verses, prophecy students think they find reference to the United States.

" 'And I shall send fire upon Magog and those who inhabit the coastlands in safety; and they will know that I am the LORD' " (v. 6).

Since America is one of the great superpowers it is natural, I suppose, for the question to arise—What part does the United States play in all this? The expression "coastlands" is a reference to the U.S., many believe. No nation in the world lives more safe and carefree than we do. Geographically, North America is an island. Furthermore, the term "coastlands" is used elsewhere to indicate the continents of the world.

Now we look at verse 9:

"Then those who inhabit the cities of Israel will go out, and make fires with the weapons and burn them, both shields and bucklers bows and arrows, war clubs and spears and for seven years they will make fires of them."

One can be confused here about the lapse of seven years. If the first battle of Armageddon inaugurates the period of the great tribulations, which is known to be seven years, how can Israel be using the discarded weapons and armament of her enemies for firewood for seven years? I believe the explanation is that the second battle will take place at the end of the seven-year tribulation and thus the burning of weapons as fuel would continue into the millennium.

Verses 11 and 12 are significant as they shed more light on details of the second battle:

"And it will come about on that day that I shall give Gog a burial ground there in Israel, the valley of those who pass by east of the sea, and it will block off the passers-by. So they will bury Gog there with all his multitude, and they will call it the valley of Hamon-gog. For seven months the house of Israel will be burying them in order to cleanse the land."

The purpose of God's intervention—the permanent spiritual awakening of His people—is spoken of in 39:28,29.

"Then they will know that I am the LORD their God because I made them go into exile among the nations, and then gathered them again to their own land; and I will leave none of them there any longer. And I will not hide My face from them any longer, for I shall have poured out My Spirit on the house of Israel," declares the Lord GOD.

Since the spiritual awakening must be preceded by the restoration to the land—and that took place in 1948 and again in 1967—we eagerly await the fulfillment of the remainder of this prophecy soon. Hosea the prophet foresaw the outcome of this second battle which ushers in the millennium of Christ's earthly reign.

"In that day I will also make a covenant for them
With the beasts of the field,
The birds of the sky,
And the creeping things of the ground.
And I will abolish the bow, the sword, and war from the land,
And will make them lie down in safety.
And I will betroth you to Me forever;
Yes, I will betroth you to Me in righteousness and in justice,
In lovingkindness and in compassion,
And I will betroth you to Me in faithfulness.
Then you will know the LORD. And it will come about in that day that I
   will respond," declares the Lord.

"I will respond to the heavens, and they will respond to the earth,
And the earth will respond to the grain, to the new wine, and to the oil,
And they will respond to Jezreel.
And I will sow her for Myself in the land.
I will also have compassion on her who had not obtained compassion,
And I will say to those who were not My people,
'You are My people!' And they will say, 'Thou art my God!' "
(Hos. 2:18–23).

The Third Battle

According to Revelation 20:7–10, following the millennium the final and ultimate battle of Armageddon will be
fought. The Lord says that "Satan will be released from his
prison, and will come out to deceive the nations which are in
the four corners of the earth, Gog and Magog, to gather them
together for the war; the number of them is like the sand of the
seashore. And they came up on the broad plain of the earth and
surrounded the camp of the saints and the beloved city, and fire
came down from heaven and devoured them."

Although it is not named, the "broad plain" would fit
exactly with the description of the plain of Megiddo. The
"beloved city" could be none other than Jerusalem. Evidently,
Satan marshals his demonic forces for a final, great battle
against the Lord Jesus Christ's "saints." At that instant,
God's Son intervenes and brings to pass the ultimate hope of
mankind. Satan and death and Hades are all forever destroyed!
How grateful we are to the Lord Jesus for such love and such
power!

In conclusion, Ezekiel 37–39 is seen as referring to Gog
before the millennium and John in Revelation writes of Gog
after the millennium. The apostle Peter's great prophetic passage is evidence of this third and final battle of Armageddon.

For this they willfully forget: that by the word of God the heavens
were of old, and the earth standing out of water and in the water, by

which the world that then was, being flooded with water, perished. But the heavens and the earth which now exist are kept in store by the same word, reserved for fire until the day of judgment and perdition of ungodly men. But, beloved, do not forget this one thing, that one day is with the Lord as a thousand years, and a thousand years as one day. The Lord is not slack concerning His promise, as some count slackness, but is longsuffering toward us, not desiring that any should perish but that all should come to repentance. But the day of the Lord will come as a thief in the night, in which the heavens will pass away with a great noise, and the elements will melt with fervent heat; both the earth and the works that are in it will be burned up. Seeing then that all these things will be dissolved, what manner of persons ought you to be in holy conduct and godliness, looking for and hastening the coming of the day of God, because of which the heavens, being on fire, will be dissolved, and the elements will melt with fervent heat? Nevertheless we, according to His promise, look for new heavens and a new earth in which righteousness dwells.

(2 Pet. 3:5–13 NKJB–NT)

12
The Mystifying Millennium

And I saw an angel coming down from heaven, having the key of the abyss and a great chain in his hand. And he laid hold of the dragon, the serpent of old, who is the devil and Satan, and bound him for a thousand years, and threw him into the abyss, and shut it and sealed it over him, so that he should not deceive the nations any longer, until the thousand years were completed; after these things he must be released for a short time. And I saw thrones, and they sat upon them, and judgment was given to them. And I saw the souls of those who had been beheaded because of the testimony of Jesus and because of the word of God, and those who had not worshiped the beast or his image, and had not received the mark upon their forehead and upon their hand; and they came to life and reigned with Christ for a thousand years. The rest of the dead did not come to life until the thousand years were completed. This is the first resurrection. Blessed and holy is the one who has a part in the first resurrection; over these the second death has no power, but they will be priests of God and of Christ and will reign with Him for a thousand years. And when the thousand years are completed, Satan will be released from his prison.

(Rev. 20:1–7)

A few years ago InterVarsity Press published the book *The Meaning of the Millennium,* and on the back cover of the book were the words "Christ is coming again." Following that statement were these comments:

With this, Christians have agreed since the first century. But since the first century there have also been many disagreements. How will Christ return? When will he return? What sort of kingdom will he establish? What is the meaning of the millennium? These questions persist today.[1]

That last question—the meaning of the millennium— engages our attention now. The word *millennium* is not a biblical word. Nowhere in our Bible does it appear. It is, of course, a Latin word and it stands for one thousand. The only place it is treated in God's Word is in Revelation 20 where the words "a thousand years" appear six times within the span of seven verses. The general public has some idea of its meaning, for occasionally one hears a reference to a utopian society or a "heaven on earth" and the word "millennium" is employed to describe what is meant. In the discussion that follows, the millennium is the one-thousand-year reign of Christ upon earth.

Numerous questions come to mind, of course. Some ask, "Why will heaven on earth be only for a thousand years instead of forever?" Others inquire: "Will the millennium usher in heaven on earth, or is it somewhere else?" Still others point to the words ". . . he [the devil] must be released for a short time" and ask "Why would the devil be inactive for a thousand years and then be released when that period of time passes?" These and many other questions come to mind which neither I nor anyone else can answer to everyone's complete satisfaction. But the Word of God can help us and from it we will answer what we can.

Views of the Early Church

Tertullian (A.D. 160–240), one of the church fathers, delved into eschatology and the idea of the millennium in the second and third centuries. He was a prolific writer and is perhaps best known for his book *Against Marcion*, in which he refutes the heretical position of another contemporary within the early church. In that book Tertullian also states the belief of the second century church in the Second Coming. It is probably the earliest recorded statement on this subject outside of the New Testament Scriptures.

Tertullian saw God's revelation divided into two chief domains: the self-revelation of God through nature and His self-revelation through history. He divided history into three periods:

1. The Law and the Prophets
2. The Gospels
3. The Holy Spirit, concluding with the visible return of Jesus Christ.

From his writings church historians conclude confidently that the early church held a firm hope of Christ's return.

Augustine (A.D. 354–430), bishop of Hippo, treated the subject of the millennium in his voluminous writings. His own salvation experience preceded his writings by many years. As a young teacher of rhetoric and literature, he cared nothing for Christianity though his mother was a saintly Christian. She prayed for him daily, grieving over the immoral life her son was leading. Augustine was a libertine and rebellious in spirit. His immoral acts included fathering a child out of wedlock.

One day there was to be a church building dedicated in Hippo and his mother asked Augustine to accompany her. ''Mother, since you like to pray so much, why don't you spend the night in the building and pray for me?'' he told her. To this she consented on one condition—that he would still be there when morning came. Hippo was a seacoast town in North Africa and there was at the time one ship in port.

The next morning the godly mother could not find her son. He had boarded the ship which by then was out at sea. But her prayers followed the young man.

In Milan, Italy, where the ship docked, Augustine sought out Ambrose who had a reputation for his brilliant oratory. Ambrose was also a pastor. Augustine was so intrigued with literature and speech that he went to the church to hear Ambrose and there he was captivated by Ambrose's eloquence. Augustine returned again and again and before long was gloriously converted. After some time he returned home to Hippo, a changed man. So changed was he that when his former paramour tried to allure him and asked, ''Augustine, Augustine, don't you remember me?'' he simply turned to her and affirmed: ''The Augustine you knew has died and is buried. You are looking at another Augustine.'' This man of learning, for whom his mother had prayed thirty years, became one of the great theologians of Christianity.

Augustine thought that the thousand years of Revelation 20 were to be understood symbolically. He did not take the period in a literal sense, indicating that a span of time would pass between the first coming of Christ and the Second Coming; Jesus would come again in His own time; therefore the millennium was to be taken symbolically.

The Amillennial View

One of the three predominant schools of thought concerning the millennium is called ''amillennialism'' because its adherents do not believe a literal thousand-year reign is taught in Scripture. In this group's thought Augustine's interpretation persists until today.

Robert G. Clouse gives a helpful, brief definition of this view:

Amillennialists hold that the Bible does not predict a period of universal peace and righteousness before the end of the world. They believe that there will be a continuous growth of good and evil in the world which will culminate in the Second Coming of Christ when the dead shall be raised and the last judgment held. Amillennialists hold that the kingdom of God is now present in the world as the victorious Christ is ruling his people by his Word and Spirit, though they also look forward to a future glorious and perfect kingdom on the new earth in the life to come. Amillennialists interpret the millennium mentioned in Revelation 20 as describing the present reign of the souls of deceased believers with Christ in heaven.[2]

The Postmillennial View

As its name implies, the postmillennial view holds that after a thousand years of tranquility and peace achieved by man's improvement and advances in all fields of endeavor, Christ will come. Then will follow judgment on the earth, ending time and inaugurating eternity. Clouse defines the postmillennial view this way:

The postmillennialist explains that the kingdom of God is now being extended through Christian teaching and preaching. This activity will cause the world to be Christianized and result in a long period of peace and prosperity called the millennium. The new age will not be essentially different from the present. It emerges as an increasing proportion of the world's inhabitants are converted to Christianity. Evil is not eliminated but will be reduced to a minimum as the moral and spiritual influence of Christians is heightened. The church will assume greater importance and many social, economic and educational problems will be solved. This period closes with the Second Coming of Christ, the resurrection of the dead and the final judgment.[3]

The Premillennial View

Premillennialists believe that the Second Coming will precede the thousand-year reign of Christ on earth and that then the world will be destroyed in the third battle of Armageddon. New heavens and new earth will appear out of the chaos of Armageddon. Again, Dr. Clouse's summary is helpful:

Premillennialists generally believe that the return of Christ will be preceded by certain signs such as the preaching of the gospel to all nations, a great apostasy, wars, famines, earthquakes, the appearance of the Antichrist and a great tribulation. His return will be followed by a period of peace and righteousness before the end of the world. Christ will reign as King in person or through a select group of followers. This reign, rather than being established by the conversion of individual souls over a long period of time, will come about suddenly and by overwhelming power. The Jews will be converted and will become very important during this time. Nature will also share in the millennial blessings by being abundantly productive. Even ferocious beasts will be tamed. Evil is held in check during this age by Christ who rules with "a rod of iron." However, at the end of the millennium there is a rebellion of wicked men which almost overwhelms the saints. Some premillennialists have taught that during this golden age dead believers will be resurrected with their glorified bodies to mingle freely with the rest of the inhabitants of the earth. After the millennium the non-Christian dead are raised and the eternal states of heaven and hell are established.[4]

The Reign to Come

These three are the most commonly held interpretations of the Second Coming and the millennium. True, some have held to other views. For instance, there is what is called "past-millennialism." This view teaches that the millennium began in A.D. 400 after Emperor Constantine declared that Christianity was the official state religion. The millennium was from A.D. 400–1400, the time of the church's supreme power over man and government. But this view can hardly be taken seriously. During that time the popes opposed, deposed, and appointed rulers at their whim. Bibles were few and those in existence were chained to podiums and desks, read only by priests. The common man was not even able to touch the Bible. During this so-called millennial period the Ottoman Turks overran the Middle East and controlled the whole region for four hundred turbulent years. History has called that era the Dark Ages. Surely if that period were the millennium of Christ it would merit the name the Age of Enlightenment!

When I arrived in this country some fourteen years ago I didn't know what I believed about the Second Coming. When Pastor Adrian Rogers asked me my view, I confided, ''I'm an amillennialist one day and a premillennialist the next.'' I could have said I was ''pro-millennium''—I was for it, whatever it is. I could sympathize with those who skirted any serious discussion of the question and declared they were ''pan-millennialists''—it will all pan out!

So far as I can determine, many seminary graduates are amillennial in their interpretation. But as I have studied the Word of God, I have come to believe that the arguments for a premillennial interpretation are the strongest. I am convinced, in mind and heart, that the Word of God teaches that Jesus will come in person and that He will reign here on earth for one thousand years. The destruction of the world will take place at the third battle of Armageddon when the thousand years are ended and then the new heavens and the new earth will appear out of the chaos.

I always admired a large painting in the office of the late Dr. Washington Watts, who was a professor at New Orleans Baptist Seminary. The painting depicted, as well as the artist could, exactly what Isaiah prophesied in 11:6–9:

And the wolf will dwell with the lamb,
And the leopard will lie down with the kid,

And the calf and the young lion and the fatling together;
And a little boy will lead them.
Also the cow and the bear will graze;
Their young will lie down together;
And the lion will eat straw like the ox.
And the nursing child will play by the hole of the cobra,
And the weaned child will put his hand on the viper's den.
They will not hurt or destroy in all My holy mountain,
For the earth will be full of the knowledge of the LORD
As the waters cover the sea.

That, I believe, vividly describes what it will be like here on earth during the millennium, when Christ will reign for a thousand years. It will be initiated when Christ descends bodily on the Mount of Olives as Zechariah announced 2,400 years ago:

And in that day His feet will stand on the Mount of Olives, which is in front of Jerusalem on the east; and the Mount of Olives will be split in its middle from east to west by a very large valley, so that half of the mountain will move toward the north and the other half toward the south (14:4).

We do not know when that day will come. But meanwhile, we praise the Lord that Jesus is coming again. Whether He comes for you and me at death or comes for all His true followers in the Rapture, let us heed His admonition: "Therefore be on the alert, for you do not know which day your Lord is coming" (Matt. 24:42).

Appendix

The Bible in numerous passages gives substantive information concerning the millennial reign, a magnificent time in God's supernatural plan of the ages. It will be a time of:

Universal Peace

And He will judge between many peoples
And render decisions for mighty, distant nations.
Then they will hammer their swords into plowshares
And their spears into pruning hooks;
Nation will not lift up sword against nation,
And never again will they train for war.
(Mic. 4:3)

Righteousness Will Prevail

There will be no end to the increase of His government or of peace,
On the throne of David and over his kingdom,
To establish it and to uphold it with justice and righteousness
From then on and forevermore.
The zeal of the LORD of hosts will accomplish this.
(Is. 9:7)

Also righteousness will be the belt about His loins,
And faithfulness the belt about His waist.
(Is. 11:5)

Then justice will dwell in the wilderness,
And righteousness will abide in the fertile field.
And the work of righteousness will be peace,
And the service of righteousness, quietness and confidence forever.
(Is. 32:16,17)

Holiness Will Characterize the Land and People

In that day there will be inscribed on the bells of the horses, "HOLY TO THE LORD." And the cooking pots in the LORD's house will be like the bowls before the altar. And every cooking pot in Jersulem and in Judah will be holy to the LORD of hosts; and all who sacrifice will come and take of them and boil in them. And there will no longer be a Canaanite in the house of the LORD of hosts in that day.
(Zech. 14:20,21)

Sickness Will Disappear

And on that day the deaf shall hear words of a book,
And out of their gloom and darkness the eyes of the blind shall see.
(Is. 29:18)

And no resident will say, "I am sick";
The people who dwell there will be forgiven their iniquity.
(Is. 33:24)

Then the eyes of the blind will be opened,
And the ears of the deaf will be unstopped.
Then the lame will leap like a deer,
And the tongue of the dumb will shout for joy.
For waters will break forth in the wilderness
And streams in the Arabah.
(Is. 35:5,6)

Longevity Promised

No longer will there be in it an infant who lives but a few days,
Or an old man who does not live out his days;
For the youth will die at the age of one hundred
And the one who does not reach the age of one hundred
Shall be thought accursed.
(Is. 65:20)

Adam's Curse Is Lifted

The wilderness and the desert will be glad,
And the Arabah will rejoice and blossom;
Like the crocus
It will blossom profusely
And rejoice with rejoicing and shout of joy.
The glory of Lebanon will be given to it,
The majesty of Carmel and Sharon.
They will see the glory of the LORD,
The majesty of our GOD.
(Is. 35:1,2)

Then He will give you rain for the seed which you will sow in the ground, and bread from the yield of the ground, and it will be rich and plenteous; on that day your livestock will graze in a roomy pasture. Also the oxen and the donkeys which work the ground will eat salted fodder, which has been winnowed with shovel and fork.
(Is. 30:23,24)

"Behold, days are coming," declares the LORD,
"When the plowman will overtake the reaper
And the treader of grapes him who sows seed;
When the mountains will drip sweet wine,
And all the hills will be dissolved."
(Amos 9:13)

"The wolf and the lamb shall graze together, and the lion shall eat straw like the ox; and dust shall be the serpent's food. They shall do

no evil or harm in all My holy mountain,'' says the LORD.
(Is. 65:25)

The Universe Is Under the Reign of Christ

Therefore also God highly exalted Him, and bestowed on Him the name which is above every name, that at the name of Jesus every knee should bow, of those who are in heaven, and on earth, and under the earth, and that every tongue should confess that Jesus Christ is Lord, to the glory of God the Father.
(Phil. 2:9 –11)

NOTES

Chapter 1

1. "Apocalypse Now?" *USA Today,* June 1980, p. 1.
2. "Doomsday Clock: Mankind near Midnight," *Futurist,* June 1980.
3. Ken Auletta, "War & Peace: the No. 1 issue—and a dilemma," New York *Daily News,* October 19, 1980, p. 34.

Chapter 2

1. Charles F. Pfeiffer, *The Dead Sea Scrolls and the Bible* (Grand Rapids: Baker Book House, 1969), p. 129.
2. Josh McDowell, *Evidence That Demands a Verdict* (San Bernardino: Campus Crusade for Christ, 1972), p. 56.
3. Matthew Poole, *A Commentary on the Holy Bible,* Vol. 1, (London: Banner of Truth Trust, 1962), p. 10.
4. D. Guthrie and J. A. Motyer, *The New Bible Commentary Revised* (Grand Rapids: Wm. B. Eerdmans, 1970), p. 113.
5. Ibid., p. 221.

Chapter 3

1. Wilbur M. Smith, *Egypt and Israel: Coming Together?* (Wheaton: Tyndale House, 1978), p. xi.
2. The *World Book Encyclopedia,* Vol. 10 (Chicago: Field Enterprises Educational Corporation, 1977), p. 388d.
3. *The Courier-News* (Bridgewater, N.J.), September 24, 1980.
4. *The Chosen People* (New York), December 1967, p. 5.
5. Jerry Falwell, *Listen, America!* (New York: Doubleday, 1980), pp. 118, 119.

Chapter 4

1. *Mobile* (Ala.) *Press,* June 16, 1977.
2. "New Light on the Ancient Temple of Jerusalem," *Christian News from Israel,* No. 2 (1979): 54–58.
3. G. Frederick Owen, *Jerusalem* (Kansas City: Beacon Hill Press, 1972), p. 127.
4. "Israel Approves Plan To Build Canal Through Gaza Strip," *The Atlanta Journal,* August 25, 1980.

Chapter 5

1. *The Arab World,* Arab Information Center, 747 Third Ave., New York, N.Y., 10017.
2. Wilbur M. Smith, *Egypt and Israel: Coming Together?* (Wheaton: Tyndale House, 1978), p. 1.
3. "Open Tunnel under Suez Canal," *The Daily News* (New York), Oct. 26, 1980.
4. "Arabic Language and Script," a publication of the Arab Information Center, New York.
5. Rom Landau, *The Arab Heritage of Western Civilization* (as quoted in a brochure made available by the Arab Information Center).

Chapter 7

1. *The Chosen People* (New York), December 1967, p. 4.

Chapter 9

1. Svetlana Aliluyeva, *Twenty Letters to a Friend* (New York: Harper & Row, 1967).
2. "The Darker Side of Sun Moon," *Time,* June 14, 1976.

Chapter 10

1. *The Criswell Study Bible* (Nashville: Thomas Nelson, 1979), p. 994.

Chapter 11

1. Hal Lindsey, *The Late Great Planet Earth* (Grand Rapids: Zondervan, 1970), p. 164.
2. *The Scofield Reference Bible* (New York: Oxford University Press, 1909), p. 883.

Chapter 12

1. Robert G. Clouse, ed., *The Meaning of the Millennium* (Downers Grove: InterVarsity, 1977).
2. Ibid., p. 9.
3. Ibid., p. 8.
4. Ibid., pp. 7, 8.

Bibliography

Periodicals

The Alabama Baptist, Alabama Baptist Convention, Birmingham, Alabama, February 14, 1979.

Christian Life, Christian Life Inc., Wheaton, Illinois, May, 1974 Issue; February, 1976 issue.

The Commission, The Foreign Mission Board of the Southern Baptist Convention, Richmond, Virginia, 1970 through February, 1979.

Eternity, Evangelical Ministries, Inc., Philadelphia, Pennsylvania, May, 1974.

Moody Monthly, Moody Bible Institute, Chicago, Illinois, March, 1974.

New York Times, Time Inc., New York, New York, October 2, 1970.

Time, Time Inc., New York, New York, Selected issues from 1967 through 1977.

Books

Anderson, Roy Allan and Hoffman, Jay Milton, *All Eyes on Israel.* Fort Worth, Texas: Harvest Press, Inc., 1976.

Atlas of the Bible Lands, Harry T. Frank, ed. Maplewood, New Jersey: Hammond Inc., 1977.

Avi-Yonah, Michael, et al., *Archaeology.* Jerusalem: Keter Publishing House, 1974.

Avi-Yonah, Michael, *The Holy Land.* London: Thames and Hudson, 1972.

Avi-Yonah, Michael, et al., *Views of the Biblical World.* 5 vols. Jerusalem-Ramat Gan.: International Publishing Company, Ltd., 1961.

Bishko, Herbert, *Look at Jerusalem.* Jerusalem, Palphot, Ltd. n.d.

Cragg, Kenneth, *Sandals at the Mosque.* New York: Oxford University Press, 1959.

Cribb, C. C., *Armageddon Dead Ahead,* Raleigh, North Carolina: Manhattan, Ltd. Publishers, 1977.

DeHaan, Richard W., *Israel and the Nations in Prophecy.* Grand Rapids: Zondervan, 1968.

Dehan, Emmanuel, *Our Visit to Israel.* Tel Aviv: Emmanuel Dehan, 1973.

Duncan, Alistair, *The Noble Sanctuary.* London: Longman Group Limited, 1972.

Eddleman, H. Leo, *Last Things.* Grand Rapids: Zondervan, 1969.

Eddleman, H. Leo, *The Second Coming.* Nashville: Broadman Press, 1963.

Fehr, Dr. Edward, *Prophetic Bible Course.* Hoisington, Kansas: Prophetic Conference Bureau, 1950.

Fodor, Eugene, *Fodor's Israel 1973.* New York: David McKay Company, Inc., 1973.

Fried, Ralph, *Reaching Arabs for Christ.* Grand Rapids: Zondervan, 1947.

Gaster, Theodor H., *The Dead Sea Scriptures.* Garden City: Doubleday, 1956.

Halley, Henry H., *Halley's Bible Handbook.* 23rd edition. Grand Rapids: Zondervan, 1962.

Harding, G. Lankester, *The Antiquities of Jordan.* London: Lutterworth Press, 1959.

Hefley, James and Hefley, Marti, *Arabs, Christians, and Jews.* Plainfield, New Jersey: Logos International, 1978.

Hefley, James and Hefley, Marti, *The Liberated Palestinian.* Wheaton; Victor Books, 1975.

Hussein, King of Jordan, *Uneasy Lies the Head.* New York: Bernard Geis Associates, 1962.

Kirban, Salem, *The Beginning of Sorrows.* Chicago: Moody Press, 1972.

Lambert, Lance, *Israel: A Secret Documentary.* Wheaton: Tyndale House Publishers, Inc., 1975.

Lindsay, Gordon, *The Miracle of Israel.* Dallas: Christ for the Nations Publishing Company, 1970.

Lindsey, Hal, et al., *When is Jesus Coming Again?* Carol Stream, Illinois: Creation House, 1974.

Logson, S. Franklin, *Is the U.S. in Prophecy?* Grand Rapids: Zondervan, 1968.

McCall, Thomas S., and Levitt, Zola, *Satan in the Sanctuary.* Chicago: Moody Press, 1972.

Newman, Paul S., *Land of the Bible.* Norwalk, Connecticut: C. R. Gibson Company, 1974.

Odle, Joe T., *The Coming of the King.* Nashville: Broadman Press, 1974.

Roger, Jean, *The Land of Jesus.* Tel Aviv: Sadan Publishing House, 1974.

Shorrosh, Anis, *The Fig Tree.* Mobile: Anis Shorrosh Evangelistic Association, 1973.

Shorrosh, Anis, *The Ultimate Reality.* Mobile: Anis Shorrosh Evangelistic Association, 1971.

Shorrosh, Anis, *Where Jesus Walked: A Pilgrim's Guidebook.* Mobile: Anis Shorrosh Evangelistic Association, 1978.

Signs and Wonders in Rabbath-Ammon. Privately published by S. B. Kawar, Amman, Jordan, n.d.

Strauss, Lehman, *The End of This Present World.* Grand Rapids: Zondervan, 1967.

Summers, Ray, *Worthy is the Lamb.* Nashville: Broadman Press, 1951.

Tatford, Frederick A., *The Climax of the Ages: Studies in the Prophecy of Daniel.* Grand Rapids: Zondervan, 1953.

Tatford, Frederick A., *God's Program of the Ages.* Grand Rapids: Kregel Publication, 1967.

The Koran, J. M. Rodwell, trans. Everyman's Library. New York: Dutton, 1909.

Wilkerson, David, *The Vision.* New York: Pyramid Communications, Inc., 1974.

Witty, Robert G., *Signs of the Second Coming.* Nashville: Broadman Press, 1969.

The World Book Encyclopedia. Chicago: Field Enterprises Educational Corporation, 1976.

Yamamoto, J. Isamu, *The Moon Doctrine.* Downers Grove: InterVarsity, 1977.